Educating Children in Conversation with Janusz Korczak

Gunda Schneider-Flume

# Educating Children in Conversation with Janusz Korczak

Pedagogy of Respect applied in the orphanage in Warsaw
from 1912 to 1942 and the experience with Korczak's
thoughts in the author's family at the End of the 20th century

**PETER LANG**

**Bibliographic Information published by the Deutsche Nationalbibliothek**
The Deutsche Nationalbibliothek lists this publication in the Deutsche
Nationalbibliografie; detailed bibliographic data is available online at
http://dnb.d-nb.de.

**Library of Congress Cataloging-in-Publication Data**
A CIP catalog record for this book has been applied for at the Library of Congress.

Cover Image: © Friedrich Lux
Cover Design: © Olaf Gloeckler, Atelier Platen, Friedberg

ISBN 978-3-631-76342-1 (Print)
E-ISBN 978-3-631-76863-1 (E-PDF)
E-ISBN 978-3-631-76864-8 (EPUB)
E-ISBN 978-3-631-76865-5 (MOBI)
DOI 10.3726/b14703

© Peter Lang GmbH
Internationaler Verlag der Wissenschaften
Berlin 2018
All rights reserved.

Peter Lang – Berlin · Bern · Bruxelles · New York ·
Oxford · Warszawa · Wien

This publication has been peer reviewed.

www.peterlang.com

# Foreword

The thoughts about living with children that I have written down in this book have accompanied me for more than 45 years. These thoughts come from the numerous diaries in which I have written and reflected on life with our children. Janusz Korczak travelled with me as my companion from the very beginning; at first in the form of a German translation of his book "How to Love a Child" and later with the German translation of his collected works.

Korczak provoked both absolute opposition and complete agreement at the same time. I could not accept the idea of his concept the "right of the child to die". However, Korczak's understanding of life and his respect for children as people convinced me, and in the end, allowed me to understand the "child's right to die" too. Although Janusz Korczak maintained that he did not think of himself as belonging to a particular religious community, his whole being is rooted in the Judeo-Christian tradition. Life is a gift that brings forth joy and thankfulness. Particularly in observations of nature – for example a meadow – the teacher could explain this to the children in a quite worldly way.

"How to Love a Child" was written during the First World War. Korczak said of it: "I wrote this book in a field hospital under the thunder of artillery, during the war." (SW 4, 115). Korczak's last entry was in his diary in 1942, a few days before his deportation, together with the children, to the death camp at Treblinka. His pedagogy is the expression of his experiences of life with children in the summer camps at the beginning of the 20th century and, after 1912, as head of the Jewish orphanage "Dom Sierot" in Warsaw.

After the Second World War, Korczak's pedagogy was seen as a part of reform pedagogy in general. In terms of intellectual history, this was the right place for it, but it had no further effect beyond that. After 1945, there were numerous different educational programs. Korczak was forgotten in Germany with the exception of his children's book "König Hänschen I." and the award of the Peace Prize of the German Book Trade in 1972. Perhaps this is because we cannot find in Korczak's books simple recipes

or ready answers for treating the individual educational problems and for
promoting the abilities of children and adolescents.

The secret of Korczak's pedagogy, his life with children, is the respect he
gives to every child. It is this respect that allows the child to become itself.
The child does not have to fulfill any ideal or become a type, but rather it
is about recognizing the child as a person, so that it may develop freely.
Performance is not neglected, but it is not at the center of the matter. To
this extent Korczak's pedagogy motivates and is motivated by, sociopolit-
ical concerns that provide the measure of humanity within a society. As
Hartmut von Hentig noted in his Laudatio at the award of the German
Book Trade's Peace Prize, Janusz Korczak's pedagogy was political in the
sense that it promoted peace.

The American sociologist Richard Sennett – in his book "Respect in
a World of Inequality" (New York, 2002) – described respect between
those who are socially unequal as the basis for social and human coex-
istence. But respect is in short supply and, as a rule, it is only the strong
who receive respect while the weak tend to receive attention only because
of their problems and crises, in which case it is impossible for the weak
to develop self-respect. Self-respect is the product of the respect that we
are accorded by others, not for any weakness or deficit, but in its own
right. Sennett's thesis can also be applied to life with children. Children
can develop self-respect only if they are accorded respect, not because
they are weaker, but because they are who they are. This is the sociopo-
litical and human significance of Janusz Korczak's pedagogy. Korczak
does not impose a program and does not judge children on the basis of
what they are to become, but rather, accords to them respect and esteem
in their daily life. This strengthens them and brings them great joy in life.

I would like to thank Claudia Tost (MA) for reading and correcting the
original manuscript and Friedrich Lux for his picture of Korczak's meadow.
For the translation into English I would like to thank Peter Thompson/
Oxford. I would also like to thank Peter Lang publishers, and in particular,
Dr. Benjamin Kloss, for taking on this book.

The reader may imagine how many conversations, how much inspi-
ration and how many arguments with my most critical interlocutor

are to be found behind these words. It is dedicated to our children and grandchildren.[1]
Stuttgart, April 2018
Gunda Schneider-Flume

---

1 In the German edition of this work ("Kinder können fliegen") quotations are from Janusz Korczak's Complete Works Edited by Friedhelm Beiner and Erich Dautzenroth, Vols 1-16, Gütersloher Verlagshaus, 1996-2005. (Cited: SW for collected works, volume page) There is no complete collection of Korczak's writings in English as yet, although individual works are available. We have quoted from the German edition translated in English by Peter Thompson. SW 4 contains mainly the four parts of "How to love a child". SW 15 contains the so called Ghetto Diaries. GSF stands for remarks of the author.

# Contents

# Introduction

Shortly before the birth of my first child I read a book that was recommended to me, "How to Love a Child" by the Polish doctor and pedagogue Janusz Korczak. I only managed to get as far as Korczak's declaration of children's rights: "I demand a Magna Carta Libertatis as a form of basic law for the child. Perhaps there are others but I have discovered the three following basic laws:

1. The child's right to die.
2. The child's right to today.
3. The child's right to be what it is." (SW 4, 45)

Horrified, I put the book aside. "The child's right to die". I did not want to understand what that meant nor could I bear it. I had so many good concepts and plans, hopes and desires for my child's life. Death had no place amongst them. This right, as formulated by Korczak, seemed to me to be an unbearable demand. It took years of living with my children and intensive work on Korczak's central pedagogical approach before I could understand the Magna Carta Libertatis as a basic law for the child.

First I had to learn that to speak of "my" child has only very limited application and validity. Of course a mother will talk during her pregnancy about "her" child, and at the same time, she has to recognize that this child is never just "her" child, but that it has its own life, influenced by many ideas and old stories from past times and by many people both living and dead. The child is a person with its own way and with its own will that will soon be developing independently.

This insight is the beginning of respect for your child. It is the beginning of respect for a human being. This insight exists in conflict with the desire for a "comfortable" child (SW 4, 19), or, as it is called today, a "low maintenance" child.

> "Children want to laugh, to run, to be boisterous. Educator, if life is a cemetery for you then at least allow them (the children, GSF) to see it as a meadow." (SW 4, 187)

This is what Janusz Korczak says to educators, to people who live with children. It is also applicable to parents, because our understanding of life determines how we live with children. Korczak's approach to life is in harmony with his Jewish heritage and the Judaic biblical tradition. I too am committed to the biblical tradition in my interpretation of the Christian faith. What is clear with Korczak, however, is that it is not about Jewish education in the sense of induction into a religion, any more than I can say that I represent Christian education in the sense of induction into a religion. What determines our relationship with children is our understanding of life, and there is no richer source for this than the biblical tradition.

The meadow that Korczak talks of frequently provides fragrance and color, as well as room for movement and play, joy and pleasure. It promotes a spirit of discovery and invention. It is, in short, a cornucopia of possibility and freedom. Korczak was able to take pleasure in nature, in sunsets, in flowers, in campfires and glowworms, butterflies and larks, and he transmitted this pleasure to the children, in that he experienced nature with them together, observed a rainbow, looked for the stars.

Life is participation, pleasure, enjoyment, enthusiasm, as much as it is about sadness and suffering. This becomes clear in jubilation and thanks, as well as lamentation. Korczak directed his thanks and his jubilation towards God without being attached to any religious community. "Thank you, loving God, for the meadow and the beautiful sunsets, for the fresh air in the evening after a hot day of tribulation and work. Oh God, you who have made it so that the flowers give off their perfume, that the glowworms shine in the earth and that the sparkling stars shine in the heavens." (SW 15, 299)

This is what Korczak wrote in 1940 in the first part of his diary from the Warsaw ghetto in memory of his experience of nature against the reality of ghetto life, in memory of nature and the freedom it gave and of his confidence in the gift of life. He wrote this against Nietzsche's understanding of life in Zarathustra. Joy in life and thankfulness is used as a reflection against the splitting of life into two that he finds in Nietzsche's philosophies. He too learned from Zarathustra: "wise are his secrets, a burden, hard and pitiless..." While he, Korczak, learned something different from Nietzsche in Zarathustra: "on one thing we agree: the paths of the master and that of mine, the follower – were onerous. There were many more defeats than victories many twists and turns and much wasted effort and time. Wasted, however, only superficially because at the hour of judgment I stand" – unlike Nietzsche – "... in a happy meadow..." (SW 15, 298f.)

It is gratitude that makes pleasure in life possible. Life can be understood as a gift. Gratitude, pleasure in life and the gifted nature of life allowed an old Janusz Korczak to see life in the final analysis as a miraculous meadow.

Education means living with children and opening their eyes to the beauty and the possibilities that this meadow offers. This is how children are enriched, through gratitude for life and for pleasure, because pleasure and gratitude intensify life.

Children are people. They need space and time, and they have rights. They have demands, and they challenge us. They question and question, and they want answers, they want to think and to work with us. They do not wish to live in a sterile protected room reserved especially for children. Korczak discovered "that it is the first and incontrovertible right of the child to speak his mind and to have an active part in our thoughts and judgments in relation to his person." (SW 4, 45) But this is difficult for parents and educators, and for this reason children are often put into places where they cannot ask questions, express wishes and think with us, and where their right to live an autonomous and responsible life and to act and think is reduced.

Life demands responsibility. Children wish for free space, and they want to develop and realize themselves in the same way that their fathers and mothers did. They have a right to this too. They take on duties and responsibilities if we allow them to, and they find pleasure in them and grow through them.

Children have a will, their own will. Often this will stands against that of the parents or the educators. Whose will will win? Parents wish to make something out of their children. Often education is understood in the following way: a personality is formed, and a child is made into something. Ideals and examples lead the way. This is usually well meant, but when one will comes up against another, the result is not always good. To educate means to cooperate. Education is a cooperative process. Parents and educators learn through this process too and are taught by their children.

Life needs time, a lot of time. Children need time. Time is the gifted condition of life. How much time do I take for myself? How much time does the child get? Who determines this? Social models and constraints determine this. Which paths should a child take? To which institutions do we entrust it? A child must be able to function. So that it can function, we give it, over time, small rewards that encourage it. But how should children function? Certainly a child that does not function according to the needs of the educator, but rather according to its own will is difficult. But the idea that children should simply function reduces their freedom.

Education means to live together with children, because children learn and live what they experience from their parents and educators. How parents and educators live and what they tell children is the first understanding of life that flows into a child. It is in the understanding of life where we find the secret: life is a gift, it is not made by people, it is not simply a commodity and it is also not a curse, even if we do encounter this thought constantly. The biblical tradition tells us that mercy gives us space and time and keeps life from falling into nothingness. God appears as a secret in our lives. Stories tell us this. Janusz Korczak repeatedly touches on the secret of life and speaks in a peculiarly worldly way about human essence: "It is made of dust but God has found a place to live in it." (SW 4, 12)

In life, people experience acknowledgement as people. The glow on the face of a mother or a father is the first sign of recognition, and it strengthens that child and allows it to grow. It is through this look of recognition that a child develops trust towards life, towards people and towards its own responsibility. It is here that a little personality is encouraged to learn self-confidence, achievement and individuality, as well as accepting its duties. All forms of loving recognition can be seen in the words of the old story as a reflection of the love of God. People live from this recognition, from this "Yes!" that is given to them at the beginning of life.

A child encounters me as a person. It makes demands and it supports me because community enriches us. The child is a wealth of life, completeness, pleasure, but also fear and worry. What will it become? According to the biblical Christian tradition, God came to us as a child. Christians celebrate the arrival of God in the manger at Christmas. Children who do not or who are not able to fulfill any of God's conditions are actually the closest to God: "truly, I say to you, whoever does not receive the kingdom of God like a child shall not enter it" it says in the Gospel according to Mark. Children are able to take life as a gift. The question is whether adults can accept this. God is the name for the gift of life.

Children are trouble and a burden. They need time, a lot of time and strength. It is said that they limit our own career opportunities. That's not what we had in mind when we wished to have a child. Of course having a child changes the nature of your career. The question is whether the gift of a child can be seen as an enrichment and a gain.

The works of Janusz Korczak, who was born in either 1878 or 1879 as Henryk Goldzmit in Warsaw and was murdered in 1942 in Treblinka, have now been published and translated. In 1912 he gave up his career as a doctor in order to take over the leadership of the Jewish orphanage in Warsaw, which he led for 30 years. During this time, he published his observations and experiences of living together with children. He had already become well known through his socially critical contributions to journals and his children's novels.

His pedagogical influence is recognized worldwide, but Korczak does not provide any recipes. There are no recipes for living together with children. Children are people, and they must not be programmed. The most important thing is the understanding of life. This understanding of life can be stimulated in conversation with Korczak. Parents, educators and children will be enriched by it. Reading Korczak's works encouraged me in my own relationship with my children and later with my grandchildren. Occasionally, it made me stop and think in a very healing way. I have outlined my personal experiences and thoughts in this little book.

# 1 More Than Me – A Person

## 1 Children are People

A child – a miracle, this little bundle, a person, not a being that will only become a person at some point in the future, not someone we have to create first, but rather a person already, demanding of our recognition and worthy of our respect. A person who needs our love.

A child – "water, a handful of carbon, calcium, nitrogen, sulphur, phosphorus, potash, iron…" so says the doctor and pedagogue Janusz Korczak. (SW 4, 12)

> "Amongst millions of people you have given birth to something – what? — a little sprout, a speck of dust — a nothing…
>
> There is something in it that feels, asks its way in the world — suffers, desires, takes pleasure, loves, trusts, hates — believes, doubts, attracts and repels.
>
> This speck of dust embraces everything with its thought: stars and oceans, mountains and valleys… Here we have the contradiction within human essence: we come from dust but God takes up residence within us." (SW 4, 12)

It is on the basis of this insight that Korczak develops the thesis that characterizes all of his work and writings; namely, that children do not become people, but that they already are.

> "They are people and not just puppets. You can appeal to their reason, they answer us and when we speak to their hearts they can feel us. Children are people and in their souls exist the seeds of all the thoughts and feelings that we already have. This is why we have to develop those seeds and nurture their growth." (SW 9, 50)

But Janusz Korczak maintains something else: namely, the way in which children are pushed aside so that adults and their problems can take up space. In his novel "When I am Small Again", Korczak thinks and empathizes himself into the situation of the child. From the perspective of someone who has again become small he maintains that:

> "It is a bitter truth that our affairs are dealt with so quickly and peripherally that our lives, our worries and failures become, for adults, a mere appendix to our real cares. There appear to be two types of life: that of the adult, to be taken seriously and given full attention, and that of the child, seen as a mere bagatelle. They are smaller and weaker and are therefore seen as mere playthings." (SW 3, 270)

If seriousness and jollity do not belong together, then we are forced to speak of a false differentiation between "proper" and "not yet proper" people, between allegedly valid and invalid life, between someone with minor worries and the "proper" grown up concerns. It is this differentiation that is used to justify indifference towards children. Who knows how serious children's worries are and how burdensome their grievances? "Our childhood years are real years of our life". (SW 3, 271) There are no invalid lives and no invalid days and no "not yet proper people". Children are people. When it comes to the growth and development of children then a critique of the so called Jargon der Eigentlichkeit is appropriate. Children are not "invalid" at any stage of their life. Using this jargon, they are indeed often pushed to one side. But who is to say what is valid and what is invalid?

After long consideration, an eight year old child says a prayer. Carefully at first, he asks whether he is allowed to say a prayer that he had thought about for a long time "in the shower and on the way to school": "Dear God, I am happy that I'm a person, that I am not simply my thoughts, my hopes, my faith and my soul but that I'm a person, a proper person! I have often thought that on my way to school, that I am a proper person, that I am Valentine!"

A proper person, what is that? The child knows that it is not only thought and intellect, not only feeling, hope, fear, a soul, any of these things, but a proper person with everything that belongs to it, including its name. A child also notices if it is constantly thought of as "not yet a proper person." But occasionally there is happiness. He prays: "I am happy". Does he know to whom he is talking when he says his prayer? Is he aware of what has caused him to pray? Obviously he knows that he can talk of his happiness to an Other. His happiness extends beyond himself. He is a person who is more than himself. The initial sort of pleasure comes when someone looks at you, talks to you. We can see it on the face of a feeding baby when it responds to its mother's face. The beginning of the human story is the answer that comes to such a question. That is the power of children and babies. The ancients called it praise. Without God as the respondent, it is impossible to think of a child as a person.

## 2 Stories

The beginnings of the human story reaches far back "to the end of times in the past", and forward "to the end of times in the future". For all time, "eternally", it says in the biblical tradition. The history of humans is closely tied up with many other stories. No child, no person is solitary. People only become individualized and isolated by isolated and individualized adults. How many stories lead to the birth of a child? It is no coincidence that poets talk of the influence of the planets: "On the day that you were given to the world, the sun stood and greeted the planets." Many stories, nature and the environment, tradition and many people contribute to the life of a newborn child. Into every individual story the great story, which creates life and holds it and gives us joy, is breathed.

God – the name of the great story, which creates life and holds it and gives us joy. I am happy that I am a person.

But not all stories provoke joy. There are destructive stories and hateful stories amongst people, stories that limit us and take away the air we breathe, sow envy and rivalry, stories of the little daily deaths that prevent us from enjoying life, stories that deny life. How often are our children's lives shaped or destroyed like this. Under these circumstances, we don't even want to think about stories of joy.

But there are interruptions: a taste of hope, a glimmer, a new perspective. The child revives, comforted by his father or a friend who comforts him like a mother would. "Have you calmed down? Are we friends again?" That is the way a child approaches her mother, not being able to endure anger and rage. What is the story that you live out with your child?

## 3 Life – A Gift?

God – the name of the story into which life is gifted with space and time. A child, a person – a gift, a benefaction and not a product or something constructed. Biological origins and development cannot hide the miracle of the gift, gratis. That is why the unfulfilled wishes of a child weigh heavily.

But what am I to do with a child? How am I to live with it? Am I to make something of it? Am I to inform it according to my will, my desires, conceptions and hopes? Often parents have great plans for "their" child.

They prepare the ground, open up opportunities. They awaken interests and train abilities. A father will put a golf-club in his son's playpen, as in the case of Tiger Woods. They are told that if they don't practice from an early age, it will never happen. But is a child given to his parents so that it can achieve what they have never done?

Before a child can be supported in its talents and gifts through education and their path laid down for them, it is important to accept the child for what it is. Often the gift of the child is not accepted for what it is. No, thank you! that's not what we imagine for our child. That's not what we wanted! That is why even before the birth, the wishes of the parents mean that the child is formed and manipulated eugenically. People are not prepared to accept the gift for what it is. Rather, they themselves take control of the gift that is not wanted or that is not seen as good enough: sex, IQ, height, athleticism, hair color, health. My child has to be designed and calculated as precisely as possible.

There are firms that will offer to select sperm or egg cells that will meet with the precise requirements of the parents. To what ends? A whole dimension of life is lost if the gifted nature of life is ignored and replaced by the desires of the parents for a genetically optimal child. Authoritarian states, too, could do the same thing. – I am happy that I am a person?

The American philosopher and ethicist Michael J. Sandel sees in genetic optimization a "Drive to Mastery". "And what the drive to mastery misses and may even destroy is an appreciation of the gifted character of human powers and achievements. To acknowledge the giftedness of life is to recognize that our talents and powers are not wholly our own doing, despite the effort we expend to develop and to exercise them."[2]

The untouchable gift of life is destroyed by eugenic planning. The character of life itself is changed when its "giftedness" (as Sandel calls it), the fact that life is a gift, is pushed aside in favor of human intervention. The gift is forgotten. Also forgotten is the old saying: "I thank you that I have been made so wonderfully" that applies to every person, even those with disabilities. Today it is the technician who praises himself. Jean-Paul Sartre once praised himself with existential pride:

---

2    M.J. Sandel, The Case Against Perfection, Harvard 2007.

"I could not grant that one received being from without, that it was preserved by inertia, and that the impulses of the mind were the effect of earlier impulses. Born of a future expectation, I leaped ahead, luminously, in my entirety; each and every moment repeated the ceremony of my birth; I wanted to see the workings of my heart as a crackling of sparks. So why should the past have enriched me? The past had not made me. On the contrary, it was I, rising from my ashes, who plucked my memory from nothingness by an act of creation which was always being repeated."[3]

It was I who made myself. Is that the pathos of existentialist creation or madness? Soon children will have to ask their parents whether they picked out the correct genetically programmed characteristics for them. Will they praise or complain to their parental technicians about the way that they, selected by the parents, look and live?

To accept life as a gift and to accept everything that goes with it always means a recognition of the freedom: I may live. Life is not only about duty and compulsion but is also a gift and permission. To transmit these dimensions of life and to maintain them is the first duty in collaboration with children, before all training and before all encouragement. Whether or not the dimension of "I may live" given during the day has been fully recognized can only be seen in the evening on the faces of the children: I am happy that I am a person. I thank you for this beautiful day. That is the radiance that we receive, or the thanks for a mediocre day, because there were too many restrictions and disappointments.

# 4 Parents and Children

A child – a person. To address them as such is to acknowledge their value, to look at them with brightness and radiance provokes the first smile. Space and time, in which a child can flourish, are given to us. What will we do with them?

## 4.1 My Child – My Property

I protect my child because it is the apple of my eye. I watch over its development and keep all bad influences from him. Janusz Korczak tells how

---

3    Jean-Paul Sartre, The Words, New York, 1964.

he, as the son of an old wealthy family of lawyers living in a beautiful flat in a "good" house in Warsaw, was not allowed to play in the yard with the caretaker's children. In Korczak's pedagogy and life, this had quite a different outcome to the one his parents intended. This warning that children should not play with other children was around not only in the 1880s. "Do not play with the kids on the street" was the refrain of a song in the 1960s intended to criticize the conventional mentality of a society which separated children. The thinking was that as a parent I have to protect my child from any negative influences. That is my responsibility. I will not leave any stone unturned when it comes to getting the best for my child. I decide, I know what is right, and if I don't I will select the most competent adviser to assist me. I determine the exact timetable for my child's day. I select the most excellent school, the most appropriate hobbies, the correct career path. I only want what is best after all. Does that work? Fear is the éminence grise in the search for the very best path through life.

Does the child itself have a say? Will it rebel against such a complete and apparently perfect environment? Will it wish to have its own adventures, make its own decisions? Is it allowed its own space and time? It is my child, after all.

## 4.2 A Child – A Heavy Burden

"When I was six weeks old I was taken to the kindergarten, and it didn't do me any harm at all. I could be dropped off at any time between six in the morning and six at night, sometimes even at weekends. Now I can't find a place at kindergarten for my six month old child. How am I supposed to manage? I don't have time" lamented a young female student. That is the complaint of a mother for whom the child is a heavy burden, a much too heavy burden. The idea of time as a gift remains an illusion, and the mother or the father become examples of people carrying a heavy burden with a child in a rucksack. "Rucksack parents" and "rucksack children"; you can see the burden written on their faces. No time to play, no time to work, no time to live. Can a child be freed from the entrapment of "no time"? Or will it be neglected because there is no time? It is difficult to understand the difficulty of integrating study or work and looking after a small child. But why is it always the children who have to carry the burden of this, whose time is taken from them and who are not given time for themselves in return? A child's life takes up a lot of time in order for it to live and play.

Children become street kids "because there are no adults who had the time to care for them and to tell them what is right and what is wrong." Korczak has the young boy Wladek come to this conclusion in his story "Glory" (First edition 1913; SW 10, 282).[4] Wladek, who is no longer able to go to school because of his father's unemployment, has to look after his younger siblings. Rather than do that, however, he takes lessons with his friend Olek and earns money in the soap factory. This means that he neglects his younger siblings. Out of necessity, the children decide to form a "League of the Knights of Honor", a self-help organization for the care and education of street kids. This seems very optimistic, maybe indeed even utopian. Korczak wishes to promote children's independence with this story, which gives the children life and their time rules and frees them from the neglect of adults. This children's novel ends with the command: "Children! You must have great goals and great dreams, and you must always strive for glory. Something will always come of it." (SW 10, 299)

## 4.3 A Child as Self-realization

"This experience, too, can be of use to me: a pregnancy and a child." This is what a successful young businesswoman reported. Her own child was to contribute to her success, her career and her self-realization. The question is whether the sight of this young baby could change her perspective on the gifted nature of the child and whether it could be fitted into the needs of her career biography?

Parents are often proud of their children, and sometimes the children contribute to the self-realization of their parents, but they are damaged if that is their only role. How much strength, effort and time parents often dedicate to their children. But children are themselves people. They need their own time and they have to be able to realize their own goals. Children are people, independent of their parents and teachers. Have we not seen how a child of around two and a half years old will use all the wild, physical

---

4   Cf Silvia Ungermann. Die Pädagogik Janusz Korczaks. Theoretische Grundlegung und praktische Verwirklichung 1896–1942, Gütersloh 2006, 219.

power available to him to try to say: "me do it!" I am much more than you think. I, too, have a will.

## 4.4 A Child – A Coincidence

A child arrives, unplanned, often unwanted; these are the coincidences that people create. A child takes up your life. Time and space are accorded to him, and you must accord time and space to him. It will confound your plans. How will you deal with that? Will the child experience love? Will you realize that bringing up a child means living together? Nothing more than that, but also nothing less.

## 5 "I Don't Know."

" 'I don't know' – in all fields of knowledge this is the primeval mist out of which all newly formed thoughts emerge and feel their way towards the truth. 'I don't know' is, for those unfamiliar with the scientific approach, pure torture." But: "The creative 'I don't know' of the modern knowledge of children is wonderful, full of life, full of beautiful surprises – and I wish to teach you how to understand it and to love it." (SW 4, 10)[5]

That is the creed of the doctor and pedagogue Janusz Korczak: "I don't know". Reverence for the child as for the adult is contained within this "I don't know". The child is the unknown quantity. Korczak greets every child with questions, wishing to know more from each authentic conversation. A child is much more than our conception of the childlike ego.

We are much more used to the alternative, "I know my child. I know what it thinks and feels. I know what my child wants and what it needs." This is the all-knowing authority of parents and educators who think they know everything about their child and what they should want. In more general terms we hear, "I know what children are like." This is a judgement that allows adults to protect themselves from surprises, a prejudice that prevents any authentic conversation with children taking place, because if we know everything there is to know, we can no longer approach a child with a questioning and open mind. As a rule, children feel this and in order

---

5   Cf Friedhelm Beiner, Was Kindern zusteht. Janusz Korczaks Pädagogik der Achtung. Inhalt-Methoden - Chancen, Gütersloh 2008, 100f.

to keep things simple, give only the answer that is expected of them. They take on the juvenile role of the child. But children are people.

## 6 The Child as Mystery

"I don't know". With this contention Korczak expresses his respect for the mystery that is the child. The question is whether parents and educators are prepared to expend the time waiting for the mystery to be revealed.? Secrets need time. Or will the adults make the quick decision for "their" child, to form them and to determine their future? Children seek freedom.

As with every other person, a child lives according to gifts that are beyond the comprehension of parents and educators. Korczak said as much in his speech to those pupils leaving the orphanage:

> "We are saying goodbye to all those who have either just left us or will soon be leaving us and not returning. We are saying goodbye at the start of a long journey. This JOURNEY is called LIFE. Many times we have thought about how we are to say goodbye to them, what advice we should give. Unfortunately words are poor and weak. We can give you nothing.
> We cannot give you GOD, because only you can find HIM in your own soul, through your own efforts.
> We cannot give you a FATHERLAND, because only you can make the effort to find it in your hearts and in your thoughts.
> We cannot give you love for your fellow man, because there can be no love without forgiveness and to forgive is difficult. It is an effort that each must make for himself.
> We give you one thing: a passion for a better life that is not possible but which may exist in the future, a passion for a life of TRUTH and JUSTICE.
> Maybe this passion will lead you to GOD and to a FATHERLAND and to LOVE. Fare well, do not forget it." (Berichte und Geschichten aus den Waisenhäusern. Aus dem Dom Seriot 1913–1926; SW 13, 370)

These words were addressed to children who were leaving the orphanage after years of good care and preparation for life and heading into independence. They were 14 or 15 years old and were starting their apprenticeships. The transition was not always successful. There was criticism that the children had not been prepared well enough for life outside the oasis of the orphanage. Outside Dom Sierot, justice was not as well served as it had been in the orphanage. But should we prepare adolescents for coming injustices by tolerating and practicing injustice at an earlier age? Should we train children in the absence of love and the presence of wickedness by initiating them into these experiences and withdrawing love from them? Or should the amount of justice, love and respect be enough to last them a lifetime, so that they can remember it and call it up to change their life experiences? Janusz Korczak took this second route and most of his pupils thanked him for it. There can be no such thing as too much justice, love and respect in childhood. In this way, children are enabled to find their own path in life.

The coming together of God, fatherland and love that was customary in the early 20th century is today – because of the many misuses of love of country for nationalist ends – disconcerting. We do not have to agree with Korczak on this point.

But Korczak's words remind us today that parents and educators cannot and should not provide guarantees for the "success" of their child's paths through life. A child lives through unknown gifts. To the grief of pragmatists, the mystery of a human being cannot be planned. Children are "more than me". They live in the stories of their time and in the world, as well as in the great story that gives us both time and space. That is what gives them their freedom. "I am happy to be a person!"

In Korczak's farewell speech to the children about to become adults, God is mentioned as a marginal concept, near to the philosophical tradition: god, the big all-doer far away in heaven. This is not the concept of the biblical tradition, where the stories tell of mercy, grace and justice. But even a marginal concept can be called up and changed later in life when necessary. People do not pray every day, but if we experience prayer once in our life then it will be there when it is needed. The memory of a marginal concept can also be filled with living experience. God's story also contains within it the so-called godless times.

# 2 The Pedagogy of Respect

## 1 Notes on Korczak's Biography[6]

Prior to his medical studies, Janusz Korczak, as a teacher, had contact with children. In 1904 he took part in a so-called summer colony as an educator. It took needy children from the big cities, from their attics and their cellars in the poor quarters of Warsaw to give them recreation in the country.

This is when Korczak first made his observations about the effect of nature on the children from the backyards of Warsaw. In his description of watching a rainbow together, we find the following:

> " 'What is that?' they ask. 'A rainbow'. They lift their heads and look: pretty – remarkable, very remarkable. The children are silent. For a moment there is complete quiet and none of the children breaks it with a word or a cry. A colorful ribbon stands in a complete semicircle high in the heavens. A triumphal arch. 'What is a rainbow? Where does it come from? What is it for?' " (SW 10, 9)

While living with children, observations and experience of nature were important to Korczak. For him, to experience nature was to experience God. Of course, we cannot draw the conclusion from this that he agreed with Spinoza's concept of God. On the other hand, it was his thankfulness – in this case for the beauty of nature – that led him to experience God.

In 1905 Korczak became the ward doctor in the Berson-Baumann children's infirmary in Warsaw. The infirmary was for needy children of the Jewish faith, who were treated and counseled for free. This was interspersed with periods as a student in Berlin, Paris and London.

In 1912 Korczak gave up his job in the hospital and took up the leadership of the Jewish orphanage "Dom Sierot". In a speech on the opening of Dom Sierot, he justified his decision with the following words: "We know the sick child, but we must also get to know that child in its healthy development. We know of genetic illnesses or minor behavioral disturbances, about which we are unable to make judgments. We only know small segments, fractions of the child's life. We have to get to know the child in all contexts,

---

6    Cf especially: F. Beiner, Janusz Korczak, Themen seines Lebens. Eine Werkbiographie, Gütersloh, 2011.

in the transition from the first to the second childhood and on to maturity, in all its shades and all its mental and physical development." (SW 4, 31) During his years in both medicine and pedagogy, Korczak published pedagogical and socially critical articles. His "Pedagogy of Respect" developed out of his contact with children.[7]

Korczak, who was a renowned specialist for children's medicine, was respected by the wealthy families of Warsaw. The dangers of an over attentive upbringing within a wealthy family became clear to him. The "over parenting" or helicopter parenting that we are familiar with today was already normal in many Warsaw families at the beginning of the 20th century. Korczak's main activity as a pedagogue was with underprivileged children. As someone who, as a child, was not allowed to play with the children in the backyards he made it his business already as a young student and afterwards as a doctor and a pedagogue to get to know the living conditions of the street kids. He knew the backyards and the rundown quarters of the big city. Korczak demanded respect for all children, seeing them as persons in their own right.

*Dom Sierot*
*Krochmalna 92*

---

7    Cf Beiner, Was Kindern zusteht (fn 5).

During the First World War, Korczak was enlisted as a doctor into the Russian army (Warsaw was under Russian rule at that time). During his time in the military, he wrote up his experiences with the education of children. In 1919 his tetralogy "How to Love a Child" appeared. Made up of four parts: the child within the family; at residential school; at summer school; Dom Sierot (orphanage), Korczak said of the writing of his book: "I wrote it in a field hospital under the thunder of artillery, during the war." (SW 4, 115)

## 2 The Child's Right to Die

"For fear that death could tear the child from our arms, we tear the child from its life. We do not want the child to die, and we therefore do not allow it to live." (SW 4, 49) Korczak's experience with over-parented children from wealthy families led to the formulation of his first right of the child. "We must take care that, because we wish to protect the child from the diphtheria bacillus, we do not keep it locked in the stuffy air of boredom and inertness." (SW 4, 47) Parents build protective walls around their children out of fear of the risk they might injure themselves, and these walls prevent children from having their own experiences – that was true at the beginning of the 20th century in wealthy Warsaw families as much as it is today in a wealthy Germany. Perhaps today, in the 21st-century, we are not as scared of bacteria as we were, but there are plenty of other measures that parents can reach for in order to lock their children away behind health and safety regulations so that they become unable to learn how to deal with danger for themselves.

In 1973(!) a four-year-old boy from a family of musicians said on the playground, in an anxious voice: "I am not allowed to play with the sand because I might hurt my hands and won't be able to play the violin anymore." Of course this is a rare example, but parents should ask themselves how much they forbid their children, allegedly to protect them. How many unnecessary and restrictive regulations are put in their way to prevent them from making their own experiences? Over protection damages freedom. A child needs – says Korczak – "to look outside, to feel freedom – to have an open window on the world." (SW 9, 253)

However, it is easy to misunderstand the right to die as a call to permissiveness. "So, should we allow everything? No, never, otherwise we will turn a bored slave into a bored tyrant." (SW 4, 51) Korczak was not in favor of an anti-authoritarian upbringing. On the contrary, he said,

> "After all, by forbidding things, we strengthen the will, at least in respect of self-control and denial, and only thus can we develop our spirit of adventure, by being active within a limited sphere, by developing the ability to escape from control. This is the only way to awaken the ability to become critical subjects. That has to be worth something as unique preparation for life. If we 'allow everything,' we have to take care that we don't simply follow our desires so that we are forced to suppress them again later. The first case leads to weakening of the will and the second to its poisoning." (SW 4, 51)

I think we can make a more positive case for prohibitions: a small number of rational and consequently imposed prohibitions as well as a clear "No" provide a "railing".

To live with children and bring them up means to stimulate them and protect them and to give them clearly defined free space in which they can have their own experiences. But how difficult and stressful that is! It is about recognizing that children are people and that they have the right, as children, to have their own experiences that may bring dangers. That is the reason for Korczak's tough formulation of the "Child's Right to Die."

During the years that I was bringing up my children, I was constantly reminded of this "right" when weighing up risks so that I didn't restrict them through an overzealous desire to protect them. Forbidding freedom is much less strenuous than allowing it. The preservation of the "Right to Die", the right to experience, can only be guaranteed by concentrated, attentive supervision and never by indifference.

## 3 The Child's Right to Today

Children are people, not in 20 years, but today. By staying committed to the concept of development, a child is constantly imagined at a much higher level, namely as the adult it is to become according to the idea of the teacher. Korczak, in contrast, demands that the child has a right to today. Today has its own significance and is not simply a stage on the way to a much more meaningful future. A person stands before you now, and he needs your recognition now. The present has priority over the future, in which the child may possibly have become a particular adult. Concepts of development which jump over the present rob children and adults of presence and abundance, because they discard the present in favor of a future in which real life allegedly is to take place.

I was able to learn with my children that life cannot be postponed. A differentiation into real and unreal means that you miss life. Life is lived today, or it is missed and valuable time is wasted. The present has to be recognized as such without all of the determining demands of the future, although we do occasionally wonder what is to become of this child. A little piece of the eternity of God in time is happening in moments when people make the most of the present. This does not restrict the development of the person.

"The teacher", Korczak writes, "is not duty-bound to take on responsibility for the future, but he is completely responsible for today. I know this view will be misunderstood. People think completely the opposite is true. That, in my view, is wrong, even if it is honest. But honest? Dishonest, rather. It is more comfortable to postpone responsibility, to transfer it to an obscure tomorrow than to take responsibility for every hour that passes today. The educator is indirectly responsible for the future, for society, but first of all he is responsible to his pupil for the present." (SW 9, 242) This theoretical practitioner of education is quite clear about this. "I shall doggedly stick to my defense of this principle (the right to today, GSF) ... Those who wish to jump over childhood to reach a far distant future miss their goal." (SW 9, 256)

But often there is a conflict between the parents and educators today and that of the child. That is why children are often only kept out of harm's way or pushed out of sight so that parents and educators can have their today. It is about presence and abundance now, today. You can see that in children when they are playing: absorbed, completely committed, not driven. Play is genuine life, not false life, not "only" play. "How much bitterness there is about real life and how much desire for it we find in children's play" Korczak notes. (SW 4, 85) Presence through play. And it will not harm their development.

At a party we can also see presence and abundance, as if time had stopped for a moment, as if eternity was glimpsed in pleasure or suffering, in conversation and in encounters. Every day events, too, can interrupt the flow of time. When the good Samaritan arrived, that is what happened. He did not go on his way following his prearranged plan. The sight of a man attacked by robbers interrupted him, and the man's cries moved him so he did what was necessary in that moment. This is where we see eternity within time, the present that is filled with love. In this way development, too, is brought back to life anew.

Friedhelm Beiner writes that Korczak "is not alone in the Jewish way of life and belief in his attitude to today and the way he treasures the 'moment'". He quotes Franz Rosenzweig, the "whole art of life lies in seeing within every moment the next thing, to want only the beginning and to leave the end to God ... There is always a price to pay if we see the next thing as merely a stepping stone to that which is to come. We should do the next thing as if there is nothing beyond it. And there is nothing beyond it. Even the thing after next is none of our business."[8]

This is how we find presence and abundance, the present of eternity in today's time, in the moment. Jewish and Christian biblical ideas agree on this understanding of time, on taking seriously the current moment, the primacy of the present. A commitment to today has become ever more important in my relationship with my own children, and it is out of this that power to make plans for the future arises.

## 4  The Child's Right to be What It Is

How should a child be? What should it be? Parents have plans, desires and fixed ideas and ideals about how their child should be; what it should become and when it should reach certain stages. This begins already when they are babies. When should it be able to sit and stand? When should it take its first steps? Should it be able to say a few words by now? Parents worry that another child can already walk or can already say three words even though it's a month younger than theirs. The doctor and pedagogue Janusz Korczak was completely relaxed when answering the "when questions". "When should a child walk and speak? When it can walk and speak. When should a child get its first teeth? At precisely the moment it gets its first teeth ... And a baby should sleep as many hours as it needs in order to get its sleep." (SW 4, 44) Perhaps the "truths" provided by contemporary experts do not apply to your child.

---

8    Beiner, Was Kindern zusteht (footnote 5), 35. Beiner quotes Franz Rosenzweig, Briefe und Tagebücher. Vol 2, Haag: Nijhoff 1979, 635f.

"To try to force a child to sleep when it doesn't want to sleep is an outrage. A table which gives information about how much sleep a child needs is absurd. It is easy to lay down a rule for the number of hours a child needs if one has a watch: they need to sleep without interruption until they wake up refreshed. I say refreshed, not lively. There will be times when a child needs more sleep…" (SW 4, 74)

These are the words of a pragmatic doctor and teacher who observes children first and then makes a judgement.

If you wish to avoid the battle about sleep, then it is worth trying to let a child read a picture book or to let it play a game until it says itself that it wants to go to sleep and that the light can be turned out. This can work wonders and will prevent the troublemaker getting out of bed half a dozen times with various different demands. It is not clear whether it is the game or the reading or the fact of their self-determination that brings about the miracle. In the early mornings, too, self-determination can work wonders. A child will be proud to play on its own while the adults sleep.

One has to observe children quite closely in order to find out what it is they want and to recognize what they are. It is not about imposing the teacher's goals and creating a child who is convenient for the adults. Children do not have to be compliant. Indeed, it is not the job of a teacher to create a compliant child. A child should be itself. As Korczak observes: "The whole of modern education is determined to create compliant children. It consistently strives, step-by-step, to anaesthetize, to suppress, to destroy any will and freedom and strength of character and spirit of adventure that the child possesses." (SW 4, 19) In many ways this is even more the case for the 21st-century than it was at the beginning of the 20th. The stresses and strains of employment mean that compliant, "frictionless" children are more needed than ever. But your child has its own rhythm.

The comparison of different children and the rules by which different stages of development are determined are important when it comes to diagnosis, and these are often applied to "children in general". However, when living with a child, it is about the particular child who wants to be itself and has a right to be itself. Of course parents compare their own children against each other and against others. Perhaps this child is quicker to pick things up, another is more skillful in its movements, but this has to happen with respect for the individuality of each child who it wants to be itself and should be itself.

But these comparisons can cause a deep wound in the heart and in the emotions of the child. "You could learn from…" A wound like that could last a lifetime. It poisons all relationships in a child's life, a person's life, often for a lifetime. I am not allowed to be myself but must be more like my sister and I don't want to be like that and I can't be like that. But that's how I will be measured, again and again. Am I not good enough? I am inferior to the sister to whom I am supposed to be equal. That is why I hate her, because she is always set up as an example to me. She is the good, successful child. The parents love her more and prefer her to me. How many family tragedies and how many egos destroyed beyond repair are created by such destructive comparisons?

Without a miracle, a child fixated on comparison with others will remain in the sad role of the ugly duckling for its whole life, suffering from the thought that it is of less worth than others. How could it be liberated from this role? How is it to experience the fact that it has been created in the image of God? Kindness looks down upon it, but it is not able to recognize it. Damage to his feelings has to be stopped, and the darkness in his heart has to be lifted. This did not happen to Cain. Envy weighed too heavily on him, envy of his brother that he was better and more loved. The traces of envy could be found deep within him and had a terrible effect on his life. The right of the person to their individuality as a human being stands against the damaging effects of comparison and prescriptive ideals.

## 5  A Pedagogy of Respect

Korczak demanded the right of the child to respect as quite analogous to human rights. The insight that children are people who do not become people until after they have grown up was the Leitmotif of his book, published in 1929, "The Child's Right to Respect". (SW 4, 383 – 414) In the introduction he wrote:

> "From childhood on we grow up with the idea that what is bigger is more important than what is small. … We respect and are amazed by what is big, what takes up more space. Small — that is just normal, and not interesting. Small people, small requirements, small pleasures and suffering. … a child is small, light, it is lesser. We have to bend down. We have to bow down to him." (SW 4, 385)

However, a child is still a person. Korczak took this position to an almost paradoxical level: "there are no children – there are only people. But children have a different set of concepts, a different set of experiences, different impulses, a different world of feeling. Don't forget that we do not know them." (SW 4, 147f.) That is why the first commandment of living together with children is that we observe them closely. Parents and educators do not know everything in advance. They must be prepared to discover things from children. I learned both with and from my children that mothers, too, do not know everything in advance, but that they learn from being together with their children.

Living together as a process of discovery. Korczak understood all education as being an experiment:

> "... In education everything is an experiment, an attempt. I attempt it with tenderness and with rigor, I attempt to encourage and to prevent, I attempt to accelerate and to hold back, I attempt to downplay and to exaggerate – we would not think of giving up a program of attempts in favor of a despotic dogma. The attempt must be cautious and enlightened – there must be no danger involved – and our entire system of education is such an attempt." (SW 9, 519)

For this reason Korczak demanded that all educators keep a diary. (SW 4, 260; 322) Children too were encouraged towards self-observation and reflection by keeping a diary.

Korczak's pedagogy is informed by respect for children as people. Educating means living alongside each other. It is a process involving children and parents/educators in which they educate each other. However, parents and educators have to be open and flexible and must not use their advantages over children. But how difficult it is to not use an authoritarian tone in order quickly to resolve the situation in favor of the adult. Cohabitation means sharing with each other, but mutual recognition is necessary. How often the opposite is the case: "We have arranged things so that the children disturb us as little as possible, and they don't find out who we actually are and what we do." (SW 4, 75) A game of hide and seek was interrupted one evening with the shy question, "Mummy, are you sad?" My daughter asked me and in doing so, she created a deep connection. The worlds of children and parents meet on the level of feelings.

But the right to respect does not just have to do with feelings but also with the ability of adolescents to make judgments. Korczak, as he writes in the second edition of his "How to Love a Child" (1929), discovered that,

"It is the primary and indisputable right of the child to speak his thoughts and to take an active part in our thoughts and judgements about his person. If we cultivate our own respect for children and our trust in them at the same time as they are growing in confidence and articulating their rights there will be fewer puzzles and mistakes." (SW 4, 45)[9]

Living together with children cannot be based on the model of the struggle for co-determination between unions and employers but rather on the realization of the natural right to participation. "What are we doing today?" "How can we solve this problem?" "Why is something not right, mean, unfair?" These are all questions that can be discussed with even very young children. The eagerness with which they put forward their own ideas has always surprised me. But the justified criticism of a four year old who says of an adult: "She's always shouting. She never laughs. She never looks at me" shows just how attentive a child is when it observes and judges.

From the perspective of mutuality in the education of children as well as adults, participation with one another and respect for each other led Korczak to develop democratic structures within education. In the orphanages, institutions were established that would, through the realization of the democratic rights and duties of the children, cement in place the codetermination and co-responsibility of the children. These included a parliament, an administrative council, a general assembly, a court, a public newspaper, a bulletin board, a book of thanks and apologies as well as other things.[10] Every child could make a complaint against another child or an adult if it had been decided that he had been treated unfairly. The right to complain is an important element in the co-determination of children. The children's court judges the case as presented. It is my belief that the right to raise a complaint or to complain should be a part of every family and should be taken seriously in every community of children and adults.

For Korczak, at the center of cohabitation of educators and children is the concept of forgiveness. "I look at the facts without illusion and I believe that the most important thing is that the teacher should be in a position to forgive everyone in every case. To understand everything is to forgive everything." (SW 9, 240)

---

9   This quote is noted as an addition to the second edition.
10  Beiner, Was Kindern zusteht (fn 5), 93.

Parents and teachers are able to experience what a miracle it is when we ask a child for forgiveness because we have been too quick to chastise or because we have scolded the child unfairly. To educate means to live with each other, to educate each other with mutual respect.

Forgiveness was also at the center of judgment in the children's court at Dom Sierot. One of the leading thoughts was: "If someone has done something bad it is better to forgive him... If someone has done something bad it is better to forgive him and wait until he does better." (SW 4, 274) Those are some of the core ideas in the court codex. Living with other people takes time, and it takes time to go the long way round.

> "The court must protect the quiet so that the more aggressive and obtrusive children cannot do them an injustice. The court must protect the weak so that the strong do not harm them. It must protect the conscientious and the hard-working from the chaotic and the lazy and the court must ensure order because disorder hurts the good, the quiet and the conscientious children most." (SW 4, 274)

Order and respect – including for every child's property – characterize the way each house looks to the outside world.

The children themselves learn how to take responsibility for the quiet and the weak. Among those duties that Korczak introduced was also to look after and accompany any new admissions to the orphanage. An older child is responsible for each newcomer, shows him everything and explains to him that which is difficult, looks after and reassures him if he has any worries.

In particular, Korczak demands esteem and respect when it comes to the children's feelings. In his children's novel "Wenn ich wieder klein bin (When I am small again)" from 1925 he makes the precursory remark "to adult readers": "You say 'dealing with children is stressful.' You're right. You say 'because we have to lower ourselves to their concepts.' Lower ourselves, bend down to, hunch over, reduce ourselves. You are wrong. That is not what is stressful, but rather that we have to lift ourselves up to their feelings. Lift ourselves up, elevate ourselves, stand on tiptoe in order to be able to reach them, in order not to damage them." (SW 3, 135)

How are parents and educators to respect the feelings of children, feelings of pleasure and feelings of sadness, of worry? How miserable we feel if we are now able to comfort a deeply worried child.

## 6 Sami the Elephant Seal

Sami the elephant seal was a particular favorite of all visitors to the zoo. Children, above all, but not only, crowded around its pool at feeding time. Sami had learned some tricks from its caretakers, which he repeated, grunting, in the hope that he would get some fish, which he would then swallow down with great gusto. Sami earned the interest and love of all the visitors to the zoo with his clumsy but remarkably quick movements and his inimitable noises.

One day the local paper carried the news on its front page that Sami the elephant seal had died. The cause was still unclear. There was a link to an article further on in the paper. At breakfast one morning a mother read the short report to her five-year-old son. He, too, loved to go and see Sami at feeding time. Immediately the boy began to cry and indeed his shock soon turned into a howl of bewilderment and incomprehension. The mother had not expected that response, and now she was in some difficulty, because the boy was due at preschool very soon.

What do we do when a child is consumed with emotion at an inconvenient point in the day? Are we in a position to empathize with the weight of that emotion and to set aside plans in order to console the child? Of course, that takes time, but it is only in this way that the little soul can be brought back into balance. To share the emotion is to console and to accompany someone empathetically.

Or is the time pressure more important? By shouting, we could make the child stick to the allegedly obligatory timetable. His feelings will be ignored. Of course, we could apologize for this afterwards, but the sadness would still weigh heavily. It is a heavy burden for a child.

## 7 Esteem and Respect

With his pedagogy of esteem and respect, Korczak presents an idea that the sociologist Richard Sennett calls respect and which underpins my explanations above.[11] This entails respect between people of a different

---

11 R. Sennett, Respekt im Zeitalter der Ungleichheit, Berlin 2007[2] (Original: R Sennett, Respect in a World of Inequality, New York 2002).

social status, between the socially weaker and the socially stronger. How are the weaker and the disadvantaged to accrue self-confidence and self-respect? In the orphanages Korczak gave socially disadvantaged children the space and the chance to develop self-confidence and to take on responsibility. The safe space of the Dom Sierot and respect for the rights of children inculcated so much power that most of them left the institution with enough self-respect to lead their own independent lives. I am of the view, that in families too, in living together with children, we must fully respect their independence and equally respect the rights that Korczak mentions; namely the child's right to die, its right to today and its right to be what it is. Children will always remain, to some extent, socially weaker, but through esteem and respect on the part of the stronger adults they can develop their own strengths and self-esteem for their whole lives.

Korczak writes: "for this reason I say that we should stop thinking of children in this fuzzy, tender, patronizing way and instead ask ourselves what rights they have." (SW 5, 24)

# 3 Children Can Fly

## 1 Flying

A childhood memory: Standing on a small hill and running down with my arms spread wide. I am flying. The soft meadow beneath my feet aids the feeling. I repeat the game over and over in order to hold onto the fascination. Older children perhaps play the same game on the open steps of a castle. They are flying.[12]

A young boy, barely 8 years old, writes an essay for school titled "A day at my dream school". He ends the essay by saying that he flew home. This was a good ending to an essay. He was bitterly disappointed when he read the teachers note: 'But children can't fly!" This teacher had never experienced children flying. She was fixed in an understanding of reality without fantasy. Is that realistic?

Children can overcome gravity if they get enough stimulation for their fantasy. Then they can fly They can discover impossible possibilities and can literally scale any wall, as in the biblical psalm about the strength of God: With my God I can scale any wall (Psalm 18:30). This is the strength that people need if they are trapped behind walls.

Already, during his time working in the summer schools, Korczak noticed how free the children of the Warsaw streets had become and how they recovered, physically mentally, and spiritually when they were able to experience nature and free space. I was able to observe the same phenomenon on summer vacations with my own children. The ability to move about freely awakens and supports children so that they are able to fly, physically and spiritually. According to Korczak, the worst thing about life in the ghetto, apart from the hunger, was the confinement and the absence of green spaces.

In the Warsaw ghetto, Janusz Korczak took care of children also outside of Dom Sierot. After visiting the foundling hospital in 1942, he reported

---

12 This is not about the psychopathological phenomenon that Hermann Argelander describes in his case study of a narcissistic character. Cf: H. Argelander, Der Flieger. Eine charakteranalytische Fallstudie, Frankfurt am Main 1980.

on the spiritual hunger of the starving and abandoned children. "The children are spiritually hungry. After telling them the fairytale Puss in Boots, which I dared to attempt, they asked for more." (SW 15, 245) Imagination liberates the children for a short time from their imprisonment in hunger and misery. They forget their situation. They fly.

During this time, Korczak helped to protect the psychological strengths of the children by encouraging their imagination, amongst other things through fairytales. In this way, they were able to construct utopias that they managed to keep alive against all odds. Adults tell of the same effect in the death camps through the recitation of poetry. Jorgé Semprun speaks of this happening in Buchenwald. Eli Wiesel reports it from Auschwitz.

On 18 July 1942 the children from Dom Sierot staged the fairytale-like drama "The Postmaster" by Tagore. An audience from the ghetto was invited. The fairy tale is a story about little Amal who is tied to his bed and can only see the outside world through the window. Zofia Szymańska, a doctor and child psychologist describes the effect of the play on the children:

> "The pupils of the Dom Sierot watch Amal full of admiration and take his words deep into themselves. How restricted the children are in the ghetto. In frustration, they press their little noses flat to look through the holes in the wall to see what is going on on 'the other side'. How they would love to be playing squirrels with Amal, running over the street to paddle in the cold stream and picking a whole armfuls of flowers. They have forgotten what flowers look like! With bated breath they waited with Amal for the letter from the king that was to free them. They believed with him that this letter would arrive at any minute. The news was brought to him by the girl with the flowers, and the watchman confirmed it. Amal trusted them and in expectation of freedom he sweetly fell asleep."[13]

That is more than reality. Imagination opens up new ground and carries the children away from restricted reality. Shortly after the play (on 6 August 1942) the children of Dom Sierot were deported to Treblinka. Janusz Korczak went with them.

As parents and teachers are we in a position to give our children enough spiritual nourishment for them to develop imagination and hope? People need imagination and the power to fly everywhere, and at all times when

---

13  Z Szymańska, Den versteinerten Herzen erlag er nicht ... S. Beiner, Janusz Korczak, Themen seines Lebens. (fn 6) 253f. See also Korczak in his Tagebuch - Erinerungen, SW 15, 363.

reality gets too restrictive and realism gets in the way of opportunity. Even at an age when our physical powers are declining and we can perhaps not walk any more, the power to fly that we learnt in our childhood can give us wings. The people of the biblical psalms talk of the wings of dawn.

## 2 Becoming Who I am

To become who you are is a miracle. But the path is hard. Parents and teachers know the power of defiance, of rage and anger, confusion and doubt that can pull children this way and that. There is no other way to find the path until a self is created that is able to both perceive itself and to trust its own power in a self-confident way. How important is the childlike "I don't want to!"? A five-year-old will resist its mother's plans with the words "I want to make only things that I want to make!" Already at a much younger age we hear the determined "me do it!" of a child. This has to be respected.

Psychology has had much to say about the development of the ego and about the development of identity and personality towards integrity and autonomy as well as identifying the crises and dangers that can often lead to lifelong problems. However, the development of a person is not strictly determined. There are always exceptions and anomalies.

"I think I'm beautiful" a young girl says about herself. She has become strong but also perceptive because she has noticed that her big sister cannot say that about herself. Why? Has this happiness escaped her?

Parents and teachers can only protect and strengthen the path towards a strong ego first of all through words. Humans are linguistic beings. They have to be addressed. We know that children can recognize their mother's voice in the first few hours of life. This voice nourishes them along with their mother's milk. Words surround the child, calm it and console it through the first difficulties in its young life and reassure it that life is to be trusted and good. Time and again in life people need this reassurance, from which the power to be able to fly originally emanates.

God is the name of the original addressing that calls a person into being; not only that a person should become autonomous and self-determining but also that it should become more than an I. A child should become a responsible person with a good life. The old story speaks of people being made in the image of God, able to take on responsibility and to exercise authority.

Janusz Korczak had children in Dom Sierot who had had hardly any
parental reassurance, dependability or security to allow them to find a path
through life with perspectives that would have made them responsible people.
He gave them a regular, daily reassurance, care and duties. He protected them
within a reliable order in which they could orientate themselves.

Reliable care, clear boundaries, an agenda for the day and daily chores
which were taken into account and evaluated gave the children a foothold,
a railing to hold on. Reliability and structure strengthen the ego. Structure
is the protective space in which children can find their way to independence.
The children in Dom Sierot were allowed to register a complaint if they were
harmed within the structures of the orphanage. Korczak demanded respect
for every individual child and also for the children's property. "Let us respect
the child's property and his money." (SW 4, 403) The children in Dom Sierot
often had only small stones, bird feathers or pencils as property, but they
had value and were recognized as treasure to the individual child and were
carefully looked after and protected. Property was the responsibility of an
individual and not of an all controlling mother or teacher. The prerequisite
for this is structure, because otherwise we can never find our belongings.

Korczak gave the children conditions in which encouragement and
approachability, "spiritual nourishment", reliability, daily care and struc-
tural order were experienced in the face of the unspeakable conditions of
the ghetto. Fairy tales were told, plays were put on and concerts were held.
In 1941 he introduced religious services in Dom Sierot.

Friedhelm Beiner quotes Michal Zylberberg:

"I was speechless. Everyone knew how far Korczak was from any religious
traditions. He noticed my amazement and said, without me asking a question: 'In
these special times I think that religious services in the Dom Sierot are absolutely
necessary. Prayer can help people, especially in the tragic times that we are now
experiencing. Of course no one is forced to take part in the service.' He was
talking about the pupils, who enjoyed complete religious freedom."[14]

The religious services were also spiritual nourishment that could lift the children up above daily concerns. They were allowed to fly. Above all, however,

---

14  Beiner, Janusz Korczak, Themen seines Lebens. (fn 6) 252. Zylberberg lived in
    the house on Chlodna-street, into which the Dom Sierot had to move at the
    end of 1940 until 1941. His diary entries are the basis of our knowledge about
    Korczak and the orphanage from this time.

the religious services pointed towards the foothold that existed outside the possibilities and power of the individual ego, more so than realism.

Dom Sierot had to move several times in the ghetto to ever smaller and more restrictive accommodation, although the number of children admitted was constantly rising. But even under these circumstances, a form of order was kept that gave the children some sort of orientation and allowed respect towards each individual. A massive main room with several side rooms was divided into an eating space, a classroom, a sewing room, a playroom and an isolation space for weak or sick children.[15] Zofia Szymańska describes the arrangement of this room in the following way: "A gigantic hall serves all the children as a dormitory. The different groups have been separated in a clever way with wardrobes and partitions. There is a puppet corner and also a quiet corner. A reading room was organized and there, behind a wardrobe, young boys were building something. Previously each room had its own purpose and everything was in its place. But even today there is no chaos in this gigantic hall."[16]

When I read about the order in this room I can see the contrast to the chaos of the excessive toys in many children's rooms and houses today, in which neither children nor parents can find individual things. We recognize the embarrassed and childlike admission: "I know I had it, but I don't know where it is now." That is the common complaint about the chaos of an excess of toys that have just become disposable items.

Approachability, care, individual responsibility, clear order and a reliable organization of time will allow a person to develop. That is how we become an I.

# 3  To Jump Over Boundaries

Strength is gained and tested through play. Even during the time in the ghetto Korczak provided the children with both the strength and the opportunity to play, or the children found the opportunities themselves. In May 1942 some of the children from Dom Sierot wrote a letter to the priest at All Saints' church, which was right next to the ghetto walls:

"Dear highly honored pastor, we would like to humbly request your kind permission for repeated visits to the church gardens on Saturdays as early as possible in the morning (6.30–10.30). We very much desire a little bit of fresh air and green

---

15  Beiner, Janusz Korczak, Themen seines Lebens (fn 6), 253.
16  *Ibid.*

grass. It is very sticky and uncomfortable where we are. We would like to get to know nature and to become friends with it. We will not tread on the new grass seed. We kindly request that you grant our wish."

(According to Korczak in his ghetto diary, SW 15, 333). Unfortunately, we do not know if they received an answer.

Play does not only expand boundaries but allows them to be jumped over altogether. A boy of scarcely five asks, "what is an artist?" He is not happy with the mother's answer. He replies: "An artist can do everything a little bit. I'm an artist because I can do everything a little bit. I can paint and I can write poems." We know how great the imagination of children is. It is the elixir of life, a draft of courage and a future perspective all at the same time. In it we find the desire for strength and at the same time such a desire strengthens the power of the child and its hopes.

An eight-year-old boy – exactly at the age at which they can fly – says: "I will be a scientist or composer." Of course that is utopian. But a child's utopia must never be mocked or rubbished. Utopia gives us wings and does not lead us to no place but rather awakens a strength which must be used with care and attention.

How often do parents ask themselves what is the best way to stimulate their children? Early stimulation in pre-primary children is today's mantra. Because of the worry about advancement, reputation and success of the children on their chosen pathway in life, in their future careers and in society, every day is about learning, performance, training and ability. To guarantee success in the future, it is necessary to practice and train today. Whole programs are developed to this end. There is a certain justification for this as long as the present is not ignored in favor of the future. The development of musicians and athletes proves that those who practice early can become a master. For some parents this is all that counts. For many, performance and success are the first commandments, and for some, they are the only ones.

Education then becomes not a mutual process of stimulating cooperation but a hard training program. "When you get to school, you'll have to be able to do that." "No one will help you later if you can't do it now." Fear is the negative motivator behind these threats.

The ability and the competence of the I are often considered as the only measure in the observation and evaluation of ego-identity. The power at the center of a small personality is amazing. The desire to learn and to prove their new abilities is fascinating. Parents' and teachers' ambitions often awaken the even greater ambitions of the child.

Even though I am no stranger to this ambition, I found my way onto a different path as a result of Korczak's works, as well as the influence the Christian biblical tradition had on me. A child's personality is not primarily about practice and training or ability and skills orientated towards performance and success. It is not primarily about the child's personal development: "My child is so advanced!" The child's isolated personality and identity, which have to be developed, should not be at the center of matters lest they come under the pressure of success. Something else is significant beforehand. We could call it the gifted character of life. Children are people. Nobody begins with himself, nobody develops out of himself but rather is given to himself. It is the passivity of the beginning, the daily encouragement that is expressed: "You are as you are, desired and good, independent of performance and success." That is the underlying melody in a person's life that transmits the biblical tradition. This encouragement gives a person deep trust in his own life. This is how joy, happiness in life, taking pleasure in life and deep basic confidence is won. By giving each child respect, Korczak reminded them time and again of this melody.

Elsewhere I have written about the "tyranny of the successful life"[17] and I have criticized the tendency to make performance and success the only valid approaches to life and to see life that is not highly productive and successful as invalid. The opposite is the case: "Life is valuable as a source of pleasure and joy..." Life is valuable without any conditions. This must be remembered when living together with children. The experience of the unconditional nature of a gifted life – the biblical tradition calls this grace — does not neglect success and performance. The strength of a child, of a person, grows out of the unconditional gifted abundance of life. People derive strength and productivity from acceptance, respect and care and when they are able to accept these things and pass them on. To allow oneself to be given these things and to enjoy what comes to us every day

---

17  G. Schneider-Flume, Leben ist kostbar. Wider die Tyrannei des gelingenden Lebens, Göttingen 2008³

means that from this primary passive gifted life comes the strength of a responsible person who is also able to fly beyond boundaries.

But effort, industriousness, performance and success need recognition and praise as well as occazional amazement from both parents and teachers. Indifference damages children and makes them lethargic.

## 4 Laughter

It is my opinion,that children can fly if they can laugh. Laughter liberates us from the pressures of the everyday. It allows joy to be expressed. It helps us to get over misfortunes. It removes from us the burdens that rest on us. "Have you laughed enough with your children today?" is what I often asked myself and sadly, all too often, I would have to say "No". Between the ages of around six to twelve my children were able to collapse into fits of laughter in which they egged each other on. They were simply happy. It was not silly; it was a taste of the beauty of the lightness of being.

Of course, there is silly laughter; that has to be allowed too. And there is the laughter of "Schadenfreude". We are aware of cynical laughter from adults. Children's laughter is usually liberating; it overcomes all limitations and lightens difficult situations. Teachers know how laughter can dissolve a critical situation.

In his "Early Writings on Children and Education" (1898 to 1907), Janusz Korczak composed a little poem about children's laughter:

> "Laugh little child, free and unconfined.
> Laugh with your mouth, with your eyes and with your mind.
> Your laughter gives us hope, your laughter gives us faith,
> Gives us love and gives us everything, this much I pray.
> And when I see your laughter — I love and I believe.
> It binds the faith in future
> It finds the best in man
> It sparks the deepest feelings
> Brings us close to life so dear
> The laughter of a child. Happy, bright and clear." (SW 9, 51f.)

Whether you like the poetry or not, you can read this early text as a motto for Korczak's lifework to the very end. I think I would be thankful and happy if I would have always attributed so much significance to my children's laughter.

"... A child needs the radiance of happiness and the warmth of love. Make sure he has a happy childhood and give him a good store of laughter for the long and thorny days ahead. Children should laugh. They should be happy." (SW 9, 76) These were Korczak's words later in life.

When she was still a kindergartener, my daughter, who was always able to read my facial expression – she didn't like it if I was too serious – asked: "Are we going to laugh a lot again today when we play?" A clear desire for joy and pleasure. Should laughter not be one of the highest aims in a life with children? We wait for a baby's first smile already at the age of 4 to 6 weeks! All fears and worries about this little citizen of the world are wiped away.

But laughter and joy do not come on command. The apostle Paul speaks of how joy is a gift from the spirit and inasmuch inaccessible. Children can bring about that if we fully let them.

# 4 Time – Life as Gift

## 1 The Primacy of Today

Just as structure allows us to find orientation in space, regular organization of time allows the chance of an intensive life in the present. Time is gifted life. You can read the joy of gifted time, gifted life on the faces of children. To have time now, to have time left, to have no more time, these are ways of living determined by time. It is not only in living together with children that time becomes a basic condition of life, but with them, time, allocation of time, planning and shortage of time are also the most common reasons for both joy or crisis. Children are confused by hurriedness and by agitation, which also destroys any joy in play, work and being together.

Janusz Korczak declared "the child's right to today" as one of the three basic rights of the child and that the present is the primary temporal mode of life. In doing this – whether consciously or intuitively – he followed the biblical Judeo-Christian tradition in which the present has primary significance in life. Of course in the present, we also remember the past, and the present is also the place of hope for the future. But the current moment takes priority, especially for children. Necessary planning and allocation of time looks out beyond the present and today. This is how modern labor processes function. Children, however, do not "function" in that manner. They have the enviable ability to be in the current moment indeed, to be completely immersed in it. This moment, the current day and the child's right to them, cannot be postponed to the future.

A further pointer to the primacy of now in Korczak's pedagogy is in the significance that he gives to forgiveness. Forgiveness means that he who is forgiven and is prepared to accept that forgiveness as well as he who forgives are able to start anew. A new beginning starts now or it is lost. To postpone a new beginning means to put it off indefinitely. Renewal has to happen now, at exactly the right point. In our lives with children, in our lives with other people, it is about constant new beginnings. This experience, too, is also in concordance with the biblical tradition. New beginnings for people are at the center of many Old Testament psalms as well as many messages from the New Testament: people are made anew by

God's intervention in times of trouble, and they are made anew by forgiveness or acceptance, as in the story of the prodigal son. Korczak, however, was not primarily interested in religious messages, but about the truth of the good life that he wanted to give to children for their journey. To begin anew over and over, to be allowed to begin anew, heals and enriches life. Children stand tall when, after some minor or major transgression, they are forgiven. They become new people.

I learned from both my children and from Korczak that attentive engagement with time allows us to live an intensive life. That is also the case in living together with children. By paying attention to time, we can see that education is a mutual process between children and adults. Children can help stop adults losing themselves in time, wallowing in memories or building castles in the air.

## 2 Time for Children – The Child's Time

When my son reached the age at which he became a philosopher, I learned from him what child's time meant. When he asked when we would go to the playground, I answered, "Soon!" His next question followed quickly: "Does that mean grown-up's soon or children's soon?" That is the answer of a child who has been "tested" by having to wait for a mother who apparently has so many important things to do, but it is, at the same time, a reminder to us that there is not only one but many times and different ways of perceiving time. To children, this fact is particularly significant. Now and today are important and we must not flee into the future or use those disappointing words "we'll see."

In their early years children do not live primarily on a timeline that can be measured with an hourglass or a chronometer. Children live in a time "for" or "to" something. This time is already filled with events, and its quality and tempo are determined by those events and everything they bring with them. There is a *time to* be hungry, which is announced by a baby's crying; a *time for* a smile of satisfaction; later a time to play, in which only the events of the game matter. There is a *time for* joy and a *time for* tears. Events and time are inextricably linked with each other. Even the time that we measure with a stopwatch – for example, when we are timing a child as they run around the house – is not chronometric time but rather *time to* run around the house. Ecclesiastes says of this *time for*: (Ecclesiastes

3:1) "There is a time for everything, and a season for every activity under the heaven." Ecclesiastes mentions to be born and to die, planting and harvesting, crying and laughing, grieving and dancing as events within a *time for*. Chronometric time, on the other hand, is an empty line, time that is measured and counted in the same way all over the world. All clocks keep the same time. We plan our appointments on this timeline. It is the basis of all labor processes and global communication.

In contrast to chronometric time, *time for* is the primary mode. This is presumably why children, in their early years, live predominantly, if not permanently, in this mode. They do not yet plan but live for the moment. We can immerse ourselves into this sort of time. For that reason, it is *time for* intensive play – play in which we no longer look at our watch but forget all time. Even older children are quite surprised when they experience play in which time is occasionally forgotten. They resurface with the question "oh, is that the time?" Adults, too, can experience this if they concentrate on the job on hand. Concentration needs *time for* without being rushed. The events which fill up this *time for* take over all sense of time. For that reason, it was not only impatience that led my daughter to say, at the age of two and a half, "I don't like 'soon'!" That is not only impatience towards an adult who sees the regulation of their time as more important than the wishes of a child. The wishes of the child come from their joy at play in *time for*, play and time belong together and must not be postponed.

The *time for* mode for specific events is also central to a biblical understanding of time, even if this is not the only understanding of time we find in the books of the Bible. But God's presence in time is told of in this mode. When we speak of the time of mercy or the time of salvation, the time of joy or also of anger, when we read: "for his anger lasts only a moment but his favor lasts a lifetime! Weeping may last through the night time, but joy comes with the morning" (Ps. 30:5). It is not about time as measured with an hourglass but about the experience, in which, looking back, anger and weeping only take up a moment compared with a lifetime of grace and the intensity of joy. We can say that the units of *time for* are measured on a different scale.

*Time for* is missing when we have no time, and we enjoy *time for* when we have it. *Time for* contains a piece of eternity, which gives us presence and fullness.

As we might expect in these times, there are two types of eternity.

There are the types of eternity that the ancient Greek philosophers had in mind when they spoke of an unbroken line untouched by time and the world and which floated above the world. Eternity, as told in the stories of the biblical tradition, is quite different. This eternity cannot be conceived as an unbroken line, and it cannot be seen as distinct from time and the world. Rather, it describes the eternity of the duration and extension of God's time until the end of times. This eternity occurs in time and in people's lives. Experience of eternity is the experience of God within *time for*. Even if people do not notice it, eternity breaks into time and interrupts in a healing way at a moment of encounter. Lovers know about this. Children experience this when they are taken into someone's arms with the words: "Everything will be all right." People who have been given a new start, who have been "as if born again" experience a little bit of eternity in *time for*.

If people do not have *time for,* they become anxious or ill and rush from one appointment to another or descend into boredom. Children who do not have *time for* are not able to play and become agitated. If *time for*, the fulfilled moment, is constantly disrupted by new appointments, then we not only rob the child of time and waste it, but we also destroy their power to live in the present as well as their ability to comprehend *time for* at all. Planning, appointments and timelines on the one side and abundant *time for* on the other can easily come into insoluble tension. This is a fundamental conflict not only when living with children.

# 3 Conflicted Time

*Time for* collects the thoughts of people for a purpose for which they are completely present, alert, committed. The ability to be present in the moment, with all one's faculties and to be able to concentrate on *time for* makes for an intensive life. Stress and frenzy destroy this ability. "Don't tell me that I have to hurry up" says a four-year-old when playing dress up, while at the same time getting dressed at lightning speed.

But people have to plan. Life runs along timelines. Work needs appointments. In the so called Erlebnis (experience) society's consistent time planning or time management there is often no place for a *time for,* as it interrupts and breaks up the run of time. It is necessary to have the courage to stop time now and again. We are forced to create niches in which time can be halted, so that *time for* can be experienced. This is particularly important for children, but adults, too, can benefit from it now and again. It is these interruptions that allow us to realize *time for* and to live it intensively. It is also possible to interrupt a child's day, so that it is not completely planned out. Often just a short uninterrupted game early in the morning, before all duties and perhaps even before kindergarten, will allow a child to enjoy the whole day.

Ghetto Fighters' House

I experienced the conflict between the adult's "soon" and that of the child whenever I made my plans without taking account of my children's time or when an unexpected delay had cost time. On a scheduled trip to the library to get some books my son asked me on the way back: "have we got *time for* a climb?" (He meant a climb on the climbing frame in the playground). I can feel my shame at having to say no. How often must we see that children's time and adults' time are scarcely reconcilable? However, children can manage some planned appointments, as long as afterwards there is *time to* play intensively. Then we can observe how relaxing concentration during *time for* is. It is as if commitment to *time for* intensive play rewards them with strength. Is it not the same for adults if they can fully concentrate on what they are doing?

In contrast, we see the tiredness that is caused by doing nothing and by boredom. For this reason, Korczak always warned against boredom. Boredom provided the basis for careful research:

> "Boredom, loneliness, and the absence of stimulation; boredom as the product of overstimulation; or too much noise, confusion. Boredom: You mustn't do that, wait, be careful, that's not very nice, these are all boring. The boredom of the new dress; the boredom of inhibition and embarrassment; the boredom of instructions, prohibitions and duties. The order is like a feverish sickness, an infected and enduring sickness that only gets worse." (SW 4, 85)

Everything that prevents *time for* becoming intensively realized, leads to boredom, that endlessly long time that seems to drag on. Korczak describes the physical manifestation of a bored child as if it were sickness:

> "Boredom in the form of apathy, indifference to any stimulation, reduced mobility, inability to communicate, lack of enthusiasm. The child gets up with reluctance, slumps over, scuffs around, stretches and yawns, answers only with mimetic gesture and monosyllables in a quiet voice and unwilling pulls a face. He demands nothing and yet is hostile towards any request. Sporadic and sudden flashes of temper, scarcely motivated, incomprehensible." (SW 4, 85)

An absence of *time for* causes a lack of concentration and as a result:

> "Boredom, increased restlessness. It (the child) cannot sit in one place, flits from one thing to another, is moody, undisciplined, naughty, aggressive, burdensome and at the same time easily insulted, cries and becomes angry. Sometimes it deliberately makes a scene just in order to receive the attention through punishment that it desires." (SW 4, 86)

Perhaps today, we should first of all ask in the case of children showing behavioral problems about the way that time is used at home before we diagnose them and reach for medication.

Conflict about time is a conflict between children and adults, but it is also a conflict for every individual during their entire lives. Where and how can we be fully immersed and enthused by something and when is time simply misused, "wasted"? The desire for *time for* these days is to be found in the movement towards meditation.

In every child's life the basis for dealing with time is laid down. There is no recipe for solving the conflict of time. Any attempt to find a work-life balance involving children is particularly difficult if our working hours are not flexible. But we can say that if it is possible to find a balance between a planned timetable with its appointments on the one side and *time for* on the other in which there is *time to* play and *time for* concentration children and adults can experience gifted time.

# 4 Time for Celebration

Celebrations and parties are of particular significance in a life together with children. The concentration of time, e.g. when celebrating Christmas, brings with it intensive life in which we experience presence and abundance. Time stops for a moment, and something appears that cannot be found in daily life.

Children feel this very strongly and are very susceptible to the joy of parties. The daily routine is interrupted, time does not run away with us and it is not used up or "killed" in the usual way. Parties bring something quite special into the everyday.

This begins already with the preparations for a party, if we allow children to participate and not dismiss them with a "you can't do that yet", because everything has to be exactly as the adult wants it. By working together on the preparations, we also enjoy mutual happiness. Older children who are already able to get the presents ready are able to experience something of the excitement before a party, in which time is too short to have everything ready in time.

The party itself, the most intensive form of *time for*, gives us a taste of eternity in the present. Our children experienced that at Christmas when playing with the nativity figures. The youngest lined all of his toy cars up in an extended queue at the manger. That too is joy, eternity in time, a high mood. But the concentration of time within happiness at a party, can also take on another form, such as in the community feeling generated at a large feast or at a game, while playing music or dancing.

Janusz Korczak knew how to celebrate with children even during the ghetto years. The concerts and theatre plays had a festival character, and they interrupted the everyday and allowed people to forget their worries. It is reported that if there was no material or clothes for costumes, the performances were done with marionettes, so that the children's torn clothes stayed hidden behind the curtain. Pleasure at the interruption of daily life remained undiminished though.

Celebrations are *time for* intensive life and experience today, but they are also open for something that reaches above daily existance. They bring memories to life and open up a little glimmer of hope in which we wait for a different future. Time remains open, not on an endless line – that would be eternal boredom – but open for whatever comes towards us or open for Him who is coming towards us.

## 5  The Constancy of Time

Children notice early on that time passes, and that it is limited. "I wish it was still mid-day and that we could have the day again. My lifetime is getting shorter but it is still very long." A six year old can philosophize like this. He can feel the transience of time, but he comforts himself by saying "still very long". First experiences of finitude also intrude into a child's life. What is constant? What remains? These experiences can even encourage pleasure in mathematical calculation when the years that possibly remain to us are counted and the question of who will still be alive in 100 years is asked. "Maybe my children?" But even the years added up will come to an end. Children can become scared about finality, about limits.

Children can be completely scared of time too. I had the experience of a five-year-old child trying to come to terms with this fear during evening prayers with the words: "God will get it right with time." Experience and truth are contained within this prayer. As far as time is concerned, with its limits, its extent, parents cannot change anything because even they are not in charge of time. That is the experience of primary passivity when it comes to time; when it comes to the fact that time runs out and cannot be stopped. Nevertheless, time is in safe hands.

We can pray that time does not run out or suddenly breaks off. The childlike formulation of "get it right" contains within it a basic confidence that time — of whatever sort – does not pass without purpose. Belief in the constancy of time that is not susceptible to the plans of human hand or brain removes all worries about the future. God's eternal nature carries people through the dark times. As it says in Psalms 31:16. "My times are in thy hand."

Perhaps Janusz Korczak had this in mind when he introduced religious services to Dom Sierot in 1941. These were designed to work against the terrible premonitions of what was to come that were circulating in the ghetto. They were an avowal of "the Other of time" that gives constancy and foothold in time.[18]

---

18  Paul Ricoeur, Zeit und Erzählung, Vol. 1, Zeit und historische Erzählung, Münster 1988, 53 (Original P. Ricoeur, Temps et récit, Paris 1983).

# 5 On Telling Off and Responsibility

## 1 A Childlike Prayer

After singing our night-time songs at bedtime, my three and a half year old daughter would often sing them alone again later. One evening I heard how she sung the song "Do You Know How Many Stars There Are?" Her second verse went "...the Lord God makes it that no one tells us off any more." I listened more carefully and thought deeply. That was a prayer from deep in her heart. She must have heard her mother scolding, especially her big brother! It had obviously broken in on her like some sort of natural force and she was scared of it. What could she do against it? In her uncertainty she called on another authority, not directly against her own mother of course, but it was obvious who was behind the "no one". The God contained within that prayer is theologically questionable – a God who can do everything – but what is important, is that there was someone to turn to in a time of need and an authority above that of the parents to whom we could sing with such trust. In terms of biblical theology, that is also true. From here we find the hopeful expectation that everything will be better and that "no one will tell us off any more".

And what about the mother who is shamed by the childlike prayer? Was I to use the excuse of my nerves once again? My little self-confident daughter helped me to answer the question about telling off. "I don't like it at all when you tell us off."

## 2 Scolding I: The Voice Sets the Tone

Shouting is an expression of displeasure, anger, annoyance or rage. But what do I mean by expression? It's not what you say, but how you say it. If it was about a rational discussion or critical voice, then we wouldn't call it "telling off". It is no coincidence that we often compare scolding with thunder and a storm. It breaks upon us. Sometimes we don't even know the reason rightaway. As a rule, however, it is directed at somebody who has done something wrong, or who has neglected to do something in the eye of the person scolding. Is it a transgression or simply carelessness? Often the person being told off is not aware of the reason. It must be bad but is it really so bad that it can't be talked about peacefully and reasonably?

Often we shout because our own impatience takes over, and we have lost control. This is spontaneous shouting that gives our annoyance free rein. Janusz Korczak advised educators to work out a strategy to rein in this spontaneous anger, so as to take a step back and to build up an internal barrier against this spontaneous reaction. In Korczak's time, it was always about stepping back from corporal punishment. Korczak wrote of himself that "I am an absolute and irreconcilable opponent of corporal punishment. A beating is, even for adults, simply a narcotic and never a means of education. Whoever hits a child is an oppressor. It should never be done without warning and only in self-defense — once at most! — on the hand and never in anger (only if there is no other way available)." (SW 4, 427) But we know that words can hurt as much as beatings and that we often regret them afterwards.

What is the reason for your anger? Often it is the same thing over and over: untidiness, mess, unpunctuality, forgetting to do something. It is almost never about a serious transgression. Every day there is a discussion about how the room, the desk, the wardrobe looks. The fact that these subjects come up every day shows that shouting creates a bad atmosphere but is largely ineffectual. Your desire is to make the child for whom you are responsible take responsibility for themselves. But does shouting work? "I don't like it at all when you tell us off." And what if we are talking about truly serious transgressions where one child has deliberately hurt or injured another? What is the best way to get him to see the error of his ways?

Bringing up and living with children demands, above all, that we are clear about our own emotions, reactions, weaknesses and mistakes. Korczak said of himself: "I am impulsive. I am not one for either Olympian happiness or philosophical balance. That is bad, yes, but what if I can do nothing about it?" (SW 4, 167). By this, Korczak did not mean that he was giving himself free rein for uncontrolled spasms of anger. On the contrary, a recognition of our own weaknesses allows us a greater degree of self-control. This is why he asked that educators to keep a diary, that they might observe themselves and develop a strategy for self-control.

In his remarks on educational work in the orphanage, Korczak writes about the mistakes made by the teachers. Much of it is applicable to life within a family, as well. Everyone makes mistakes when living together with and educating children. I am of the opinion that knowing this reduces the sense of superiority that parents and teachers often have and allows for difference of thought. "There are mistakes that you will make many times because you are a human being and not a machine." (SW 4, 166) "You will make these mistakes because only those who do nothing make no mistakes." (SW 4, 167) "The good teacher is distinguished from the bad teacher only by the number of mistakes they make and the injustice they cause. There are mistakes that a good teacher makes only once; he considers them self critically, does not repeat them and remembers them for a long time." (SW 4, 168) These are not just self-exculpatory remarks for teachers and parents but, rather, they are designed to promote a critical attitude in teachers and parents towards themselves and their educational reactions.

Children also have to be allowed to make mistakes. "Allow children to make mistakes and also to strive in good heart to correct them. Children want to laugh and run and be carefree." It is in this context that we see the above quote: "teachers, if life for you is a cemetery then please allow them at least to see it as a meadow." (SW 4, 187)

Often children know in advance what will cause their parents or teachers to scold them. They stand there embarrassed with their heads bowed. They are the subordinate ones. By telling them off, they are occasionally literally made to feel small. Of course, there is justified scolding when we need to express our anger, but it is to be regretted if the purpose is not to hold the child accountable, but to make it feel small. In this case, the parent or educator should let the storm pass, feel oppressed and themselves develop feelings of anger and resentment. Very quickly a virtuous cycle can develop: degradation, feeling small, children's anger, teacher's or parent's anger followed by a repetition of the whole thing. Korczak's thoughts can help to break the cycle.

# 3 Responsibility

It is not our own annoyance that should be at the center of any admonishment but the question: "How can the 'naughty' child or the child who has been neglectful of its duties be encouraged to take responsibility for its own behavior and to change it?" How can he be helped to build up the strength in order to correct his own bad behavior and to improve himself? The pedagogy of respect intends to strengthen the personality of adolescents; instead of making him feel small. the idea is to strengthen a sense of responsibility.

I have seen children's diary entries that have taken the initiative in this matter. They want to change everything, above all themselves. But they wish to do that within their own sense of responsibility. The "me do it!" of the young child who, at two years old, knocks the spoon out of your hand because he wants to feed himself, can be encouraged if they are given enough space to develop their own strength and judgement. They will create their own resolutions, and thereby change themselves as well as put an end to the endless arguing, only when they have realized what the purpose of the resolution is. They wish to take themselves in hand but do not yet realize how difficult that is. "I want to be well behaved." "I don't want to be late for things anymore." "I don't want to forget what it is I have to do any more." These are the things I read in a diary. How many serious New Year resolutions I have read in adolescent diaries! "I promise!" "Never again!" "New beginning!" "Be punctual!" This is adolescent radicalism. Can parents and teachers tone this down and protect their children from failure and its following disappointment?

In Korczak's homes, the democratic institutions contributed to the development of adolescence responsibility and personality. The right to have a voice in the children's court or parliament and to make a complaint made the children self-confident, and helped them grow up. The controlled allocation of duties strengthened a sense of responsibility. How are people to exercise responsibility, including for themselves, if they do not have serious duties to carry out? I am of the opinion that overprotected children are damaged when they are constantly served rather than taking on responsibility for duties themselves, even if they make mistakes. By removing duties from children by taking everything away from them, we forget that duties are not only burdens but help to encourage children to grow up and strengthen their sense of self responsibility. Sylvia Ungermann quotes Korczak's last secretary – Igor Newerly – with the words: "The whole system (education through the democratic institutions of children's self-determination in the orphanages run by Janusz Korczak, GSF) was based on the Shakespearean appeal:[19] Restrain yourself once. That will give you the joy of the next victory."

Alina Edestin, herself a pupil at Dom Sierot, tells of a beautiful example of the duty of an older resident of the orphanage to look after newcomers.[20] On her first night in the orphanage she was completely terrified, and Korczak comforted her. Looking back, she writes: "During breakfast the next morning the doctor came to our table leading a young girl, eyes red with crying, to our table and said to me: 'This is Perelka. She is going to sit next to you at the table and from today she will also sleep next to you in the dormitory. Look, she's younger than you so you will be her older friend, look after her and help her with everything. She is new here, just like you, and doesn't know anyone yet. I am putting you in charge of her because you are a good girl and I can trust you.' And the doctor sat Perelka down next to me. There were eight of us at the table, and Perelka made nine. I looked to the other children – my new friends – and it seemed to me that they respected me. The sense of my own importance combined with satisfaction meant that my face reddened. I was proud that the doctor trusted me and was happy that he had selected me, of all people, for this special role. I moved our chairs closer together, cut her bread and so began my life in Janusz Korczak's and Stefania Wilczynska's orphanage." When we read this little autobiographical report, we can almost feel how during the described scene the body language of the small Alina Edstein must have changed. She stretches, grows taller and more proud. Without duties there is no responsibility. To complete the task of looking after someone and recognition for it, strengthens the small person's ability to become responsible.

Korczak introduced something into the homes he led that was to strengthen the initiative of the children, namely, the wager. Once a week children were allowed to enter a wager with the teachers. They bet on themselves, for example, that they would not start any fights in the coming week or that they would not swear or lie or steal.[21] The wagers were intended

---

19 Ungermann, Die Pädagogik Janusz Korczaks (footnote 5), 124.
20 Ungermann, Die Pädagogik Janusz Korczaks (footnote 5), 186f., quoted in Izrael Zyngman, Janusz Korczak in der Erinnerung von Zeitzeugen, den Bericht von Alina Edestin.
21 cf M. Falska, Umriß der Organisation der Erziehungsarbeit im 'Nasz Dom', (SW 13,547 – 563, here: 560f.).

as a way of supporting children who wanted to get out of bad habits. The teachers noted down the wagers, which were valid for a week. Korczak was always concerned that the children should not overstretch themselves in their wagers, so that they would not be disappointed with themselves later. It was not about "never again", but about small steps towards a reduction in transgression. The tough kids were not expected to give up fighting altogether but to reduce it to maybe seven times in the week. If this was achieved, there was a small reward and if not, then the child had to pay back something, perhaps two sweets. "There are a few (children, GSF), who make the same bet for many months and reduce the number of transgressions week by week. They get down to zero and then stay there for some time. Later, they are pleased to be able to say: 'I don't need to bet anymore because I have stopped doing it.' It sometimes happens that the old habits return after a time, and they are then sad and serious: 'I thought I had given it up, but I am doing the same thing again.' Then they start the same difficult path towards a systematic victory over their weakness or bad habit."[22]

Victory over oneself is universally good! To be unsuccessful in the attempt is painful and requires patient support in order to be able to make repeated attempts. It is particularly difficult, it would seem, to overcome shouting and swearing, which adolescents use to make each other feel small and to hurt each other.

Children are certainly not able to do anything about their parent's or teachers' scolding. Each person must conquer themselves because only in this way are we able to find the difficult path to becoming a responsible person. I am of the opinion that thinking about Korczak's introduction of the wager system can avoid many of the pitfalls of a scolding which considers itself to be educational. Adults will be forced to admit to themselves, however, that they will often shout even if they do not intend to. Children must be allowed to complain about it. They also deserve unconditional recognition for successful self-control. Of course there are many other ways of supporting a child in its own attempts to find resolution. There are rewards other than sweets. It has been my experience that children will

---

22  M. Falska *ibid*. (SW 13, 561).

earn the right to watch a short film if they have successfully controlled themselves. That, too, is a form of wager. But children have to be protected from overreaching themselves by claiming "never again". The recognition they derive will support them in their further efforts.

## 4 Children's Complaints

The establishment of a court at Dom Sierot led to the institutionalization of a right of complaint. The children were allowed to bring anything that had hurt them to court. For me still today, looking back on it, this is a question of conscience. Was I ready, as a mother and educator, to listen to the children's complaints and to discuss them? Were my children sufficiently allowed to complain about injustices? It is much more common to imagine that children are the ones who should be on the receiving end of criticism. Parents, on the other hand, are not to be criticized, in any case, not by their offspring. This, apparently, undermines their authority. This ignores how clarifying and supportive a conversation is in which all those involved peacefully discuss the issue at hand. Children must be allowed to complain and to object to what they think of as their parents' incorrect reactions.

On different occasions, Korczak put himself before the court and his written statements were discussed: "Once, because I gave a boy a clip round the ear and once because I threw another out of the bedroom and once when I made a boy stand at the corner..." Of this he said: "I maintain with all my power that these few cases (he speaks of five cases within six months, GSF) were the foundation for my education as a 'constitutional' pedagogue who is fair to the children not because he likes them or even loves them, but because there is an institution that will protect them from the injustice, arbitrariness and despotism of the teacher." (SW 4,312)

Within the family, there is no court and no institutionalized system of complaint and law. Does this not mean that the child's right to critically call into question the parents' actions should be all the more respected – to protect the parents from injustice, arbitrariness, despotism and rushed and unjustified shouting and to protect the children from unfair demoralization? In this way, the sense of responsibility of the children and even the authority of the parents could be supported. In the family, too, it is not about feelings but about justice. "I don't like it at all when you tell us off."

## 5 Scolding II: With a Pinch of Humor

It is always best to use a little humor when telling a child off. We can see this clearly if we look at the words that Janusz Korczak chooses. Children are easily able to perceive if language is used to make them feel small or whether there is a smile at work that the delinquent can notice.

"Sometimes it is enough to say 'oh, come on'... But more often, it is necessary to reach for a heavier frying pan with more serious expressions and sentiments. (Because there are both minimal transgressions and highly criminal activities, one must therefore have a whole cornucopia of different words at one's disposal.") (SW 4, 440).

Korczak then lists a number of carefully thought out expressions: "You know, I have observed that using the same phrases over and over reduces their effect and weakens their power... It is quite different if I thunder: 'Oh you — motorhome... you hurricane, you perpetuum mobile.' – in this way I avoid the monotony, renew my repertoire and use all sorts of different areas of expertise. From ornithology: 'oh, you crow.' From the world of music: 'Oh, you old flute – you cymbal.' We can never predict what will help. I knew one naughty little boy – I tried all sorts of different ways – nothing. I tried all sorts of nouns – nothing; until once I said: 'oh, you F major.' Afterwards he was as quiet as a little mouse trapped under a broom." (SW 4,440)

It is all about baffling the rebuked child and encouraging it to reflect. Korczak says of himself: "If, for example, I shout at someone (because I have to), I will always say afterwards: 'I will be cross with you until lunch-time'..." (SW 4, 439) Anger doesn't last forever, and it must be limited in its duration. The storm always passes.

From Korczak I have learnt to use phrases that do not make children feel small, but make them think. Once when I felt how I had hurt someone by using an unfair, unfitting word – luckily the anger was thrown right back at me – I became more careful about the phrases I chose. A Swabian swearing calendar played a big role in my family. It is printed every year and for each day there is a special swearword — sometimes funny, sometimes less funny. It hung directly next to our dining table and was used by parents and children alike. It reminded me of Korczak's warning about self-control and choosing our words carefully, even when we are angry. With the help of this

Swabian repertoire, the children were able to control their own swearing, as were the parents. I am sure that there are other collections of more or less intelligent swear words that can bring a smile to everyone's face.

## 6 Forgiving

"Are we friends again?" I often think back to this question, as asked by my children. Conflicts are there to be resolved. They should never be drawn out. "Shall we have a day tomorrow without any shouting?" my little daughter wished to be reassured. When living with children it is important that irritation and anger – as well as punishment – are not dragged around for days. Things should be cleared up as quickly as possible. It is the same when it comes to God's wrath: "For his anger lasts only a moment but his favor lasts a lifetime." (Psalms 30:6)

And what is to be done when impatience wins the upper hand? When we tell them off again? There is one medicine that works wonders: Ask the child to forgive you, because he who is asked for forgiveness is not humiliated but raised up. To ask for forgiveness is to heal all hurt and broken relationships.

# 6 Belief in God and Prayer

## 1 Prayer and Doubt

"Fundamentally, I am a doubter who hates rituals. But what has remained for me is a belief in God and prayer. I defend both of those things, because we can't live without them. Humanity cannot be the product of pure coincidence." (SW 3, 91) This was Janusz Korczak's position already as pupil in 1894, although he rejected the religion of his fellow "confessing" pupils. The joy and celebration that he expressed in memory of his experiences with nature and his thankfulness to God, as well as the deep sigh of his concern for children which he formulated in the night-time informed his prayers throughout his life. In this too, he was committed to the biblical tradition: human fear and human joy are not only to be found within the individual but have to be expressed before another, before God. It is not necessary to have a system of religious thought in order to achieve this.

Children teach us to pray when they are overwhelmed with joy or when they are struggling against an uncontrollable sense of fear and suffering. Are we able to share, to speak, to call, to cry out their joy or fear?

## 2 The Deep Sigh

We learn to pray alongside children, with all the fear that we have about them, with all the care. Who amongst us does not recognize the deep sigh: "Oh God, what is to become of this child?" It has not quite made it into the world. Will we have to give it back? We were so joyful, wanted to be happy and now this fear. Why, oh God, a sick child? What sort of life will it have? How am I to live with it? In our lives together with children we experience this deep sigh not only at the beginning, but time and time again; when we are in despair about the behavior of an adolescent; when someone has made a terrible mistake. What is to become of him? What shall I do, oh God?

The deep sigh exists where there is no knowledge and no explanation to comfort us. We experience this sigh where anger and helplessness rule. The Bible knows of these questions. Why? How long? Why, oh God? When

I no longer know the way, I call out to God.[23] This cry explains nothing and yet it opens up a narrow, closed situation with a cry out to another. You are not alone in yourself.

Living with children brings many deep sighs. Janusz Korczak tells us how a deep sigh can turn into a long complaint. In a report by Korczak from Dom Sierot we read:

"Tonight I took a long walk through the dormitories. I was sad. The boys were asleep. Only one of them woke up and looked at me surprised – he did not know why I was going around when all were sleeping peacefully. But he went back to sleep quite quickly. But I did not sleep. I prayed.

God, do you know Piotruś? Do you know how we suffered when we found out that he was stealing and encouraging others to evil deeds? We had to expel him from the Dom Sierot. And what happened? We gave him into the charge of an apprentice master – but it did not go well. They took away his bed and his soap; they were supposed to give him two grosz for every coat he looked after – but he was not paid. They know that he is an orphan and who looks out for orphans? Give me a sign, oh God. What should I do? Should I take him back? And what if he steals again and leads others into temptation?

Should we leave him where he is? And what if he says: 'they took away my soap so I don't see why I shouldn't take things from others.' Should we take him to a different master? But then we will have to tell that master that he steals. No decent master will take him and a different one will be exactly the same – perhaps even worse?

Oh God, why do we have to give children under our care to strangers? Why can it not be as we would desire it? Why?" (SW 13, 362).

"Oh God, why can we not let our children simply play in the white snow? Why can we not let them watch the stars on a still night? Why can they not take pleasure from a beautiful spring? We have to give them to strangers, to workshops where they are far from the green leaves, where their soap is taken away and they are never paid the two groszy for taking in the coats.

Oh Almighty God, tell me what I am to do with Piotruś." (Berichte und Geschichten aus den Waisenhäusern, aus dem Dom Sierot 1913–1926; SW 13, 363.)

God – a cry, prayer – a deep sigh of fear and confusion but the cry does not trail off into the void. In the Other, new paths are sought and possibilities arise. Where there appears to be no way out, a hand reaches out, searching. You search but do not fall into panic.

---

23   cf E. Jüngel: "Gott ist ein Rufwort (Mk 15, 34)." Ders. - Gott - als Wort unserer Sprache (1969), in: Ders. Unterwegs zur Sache. Theologische Bemerkungen, Tübingen, 2000, 80–104, 97.

# 3  Prayer as Space to Live

People do not have to pray and must not be forced to pray. But prayer opens a space in which we can take shelter. It is a structure into which we can integrate. My two year old grandson came to breakfast one morning and said to me, beaming: "Amen Sing!" He remembers the grace that is sung, in which the Amen is accompanied by banging on the table. The little man is not following theological debates in his memory. What is important to him, however, is the joy he felt when our Amen made the cups wobble. But even this young child had understood the order that means that meals can, time and again, be celebrated together with joy and thankfulness. We can join in prayer.

The language of the Psalms, their terms and stories provide the building blocks of a space for prayer. It is not about dogmatic formulations. It is not even about the definitions of God. In the prayers of the biblical tradition, in the Psalms, we find cheering and singing, questioning and wailing, pleading and hoping. The oceans bubble with joy and the mountains are happy. Those who pray bring their life to God, to whom they can pray even if they think they do not believe. God is the Other of human pleading and calling, holding human's wishes and fears. We call from the deep: why? Help and protection, security and shelter are prayed for and praised: "with my God I can leap over a wall." (Psalms 18:29)

We speak of justice and of truth that carries us through life and reassures us. What does that mean? "It is quite different at our school", comments a young boy, bitterly. "The boys hit you there and then they threaten to hit you again later." There is lying and treachery, false accusation and violence. These things, too, can be addressed in prayer. Strength, rescue, overcoming fear, protection – these are our wishes. But the space of prayer is not an ideal or an illusion. The individual words create a new reality in everyday life. Reassurance grows. Praying brings the Other closer. Even in abandonment, he who prays is not abandoned.

Concerns about Piotruś, who had to leave the orphanage, are reflected in evening prayers: "Almighty God, tell me what I am to do with Piotruś."

Janusz Korczak introduced morning prayers to Dom Sierot. Nobody was forced to take part. It was an offer that gave regular structure to the day. Prayer is space to live and orders the day. It gives me orientation outside myself: "When I remember you upon my bed, and meditate on you in the watches of the night." (Psalms 63:6) We can join in.

Evening prayers have a special significance. The cares, stress, worries and pleasures of the day can be addressed again. Prayer is not a blanket that covers everything and harmonizes it. Fears and lamentation as well as bitter accusation can be spoken in prayer, as can wishes and hopes. In all honesty, one is sometimes only thankful for a "mediocre" day. Where time and space are given for contemplation you are not alone with your burdens. Prayer opens free space for trust in which the burdens of the day can be laid down. A life of prayer with the Other, even if it is scarcely recognized.

## 4 God, Heaven and the Black Hole

The meaning of the word God changes with the persons praying. God and the world are different if we want to leap with joy and quite different if we are angry or sad. But it is not only our mood that changes the image of God. Concepts and thought change with time and with changes in our ability to think bringing a change in our conception of God. At first we think of God as a father who knows everything and can do everything. This is a comforting idea that children find difficult to give up. All-doer/ Omnipotence: All possibilities can be realized by God's action. Many people continue to perceive this as the only way of seeing God's omnipotence: God can do what he wants, unlimited and undeterminable.

An old dogmatic definition of God maintains that God is omnipotent, eternal, incomprehensible and infinite. These are philosophical conceptions that are linked to the biblical tradition and which were transformed there too. A God who answers our calls and who takes pity on our human concerns is defined by the power of mercy and of love. The almighty "all-doer" God cannot survive if He does not do everything and answer every desire or prevent all suffering. As a rule, people leave this concept of God behind as they grow up.

Adolescents only take on the idea of the "all doer"-omnipotence in order to be able to sharpen their criticism of God. "If there is a God why doesn't he prevent war even though you pray for peace?" Calling on God is left behind along with the idea of the "all doer" omnipotence, because we learn that realistically not everything can be done. The "all doer" God stays a distant memory from our childhood, and is often mocked.

As we pray, so our concept of God changes. God in heaven? What is heaven? "Can we ring heaven?" a three year old asks, unable to grasp that a recently deceased relative cannot be reached. "Where is God in heaven? He can't be in a black hole otherwise he would be sucked up." This is the argument of a six year old who already has a different concept of God.

Where is God? God is everywhere but not with us, so it seems. The concept of closeness is all too difficult to grasp, and yet our connection to God can only survive if we are able to turn the distant "Super"- God into a near God; the God of prayer, who speaks to us and encourages us, comforts and exhorts us, who accompanies us when He seems to be absent and who finds for us new trust in the stories we know from the biblical tradition.

## 5  Do You Know Who is Punishing You?

One use, or rather abuse, of the concept of God remains in play and cannot be abolished: A young boy came to us to play. His grandmother looked at him suspiciously, raised her index finger and warned him not to take any risks while climbing about. "You know who will punish you?" According to Swabian traditions this question is not even about a wrathful God, but a Jesus who punishes.

This functionalization of a punishing God or an angry Jesus in the process of regimenting children was known to me from a young age. After all, I grew up with the threatening announcements of an au pair who told me that God saw exactly what food I was nibbling on. This is a particularly effective technique in the run-up to Christmas, but it can have terrible consequences well beyond Christmas biscuits. Even adolescents soon reject this concept of God as laughable.

Questions about the wrath of God and his punishments and mercy and forgiveness are theologically and humanly of the greatest importance but this way of educating children and adolescents is unforgivable. It is a significant theological error if God is functionalized for the purposes of education. In the biblical tradition, God's wrath and punishment is measured against His mercifulness. Any restrictions on children are not from God. They may be strict but they must be fair.

Against mercifulness we also find in the biblical tradition the doctrine of reaping what you sow that apparently has universal application. This law explains suffering, sickness and misfortune with the guilt of the sufferer and the punishment he receives. You will receive according to how you behave. Those who are sick and suffering often take on this ancient explanation rather than believing in the arbitrariness of their suffering. Better to have an incorrect explanation than none. May we protect children from the constant repetition of the idea of reaping what you sow, so that they are protected from an understanding of life in which guilt, God's wrath and punishment is more important than goodness and mercy.

# 6 There is No God

The discussion about whether or not there is a God begins in kindergarten. "There is no God!" insists a preschool child. "My mummy tells stories about God" counters my little daughter. The eight-year-old boy comes home with the firm conviction that "there is no God"; we just talk to ourselves when we are praying. You can't touch him. He doesn't exist or we would have seen him from our spacecraft." These are the statements of ideologically committed cosmonauts that are being repeated. The old stories do not work anymore. In school, the story of Abraham is being told. "But I can imagine Abraham without God." This argument is used against many biblical stories. "The story of Paradise is only told to stop people being afraid." In this way children discover that religion is an illusion.

However, prayer remains, at least for now, untouchable. As does the desire and the search for the Other. Prayer carries us with its discipline. It gives us space to think and to reason, space for fear and worry and also for joy and acclamation.

Another variant of young peoples' denial of God is: "God is a joke figure who was invented to make the stories more exciting." This, too, was the eight-year-old's explanation. I was taken aback, but I could respond by saying that there are indeed funny stories about God, like that of the disobedient prophet Jonah, who, because of fear of the storm was thrown overboard by the sailors so that the storm would be stilled. God, according to this story, sent a big fish to swallow Jonah, so saving him. After three days and three nights he was spat up onto the land. A strange God indeed. The point of the story is that God wanted to convince Jonah of his mercifulness, even against the apostates of Nineveh. A surprising story full of comedy and an illustration of holy mercy, a new perspective in the world.

Should we not more often point towards a surprising story about God? Only in this way can the truth about God and the truth about mercy be told.

A nine-year old boy came up with a theologically well-founded criticism of an image of God when a teacher in the school tried to intimidate the children with tales of penitence and sin: "Whenever they talk like that, I always think straightaway that there is no God." Children can and must be involved in the criticism of images of God because the images grow with them.

## 7 Thankfulness Out of the Memory of Joy

At this point we need to remind ourselves of Janusz Korczak's critique of Nietzsche's understanding of life in Zarathustra. Korczak wants to give an answer to Nietzsche, because the book had done so much damage. In the first part of his diaries from the ghetto in 1940 he writes: "The same Zarathustra has taught me a different lesson (than Nietzsche, GSF)... We agree on one thing: the way of the master and that of me, the pupil – they were difficult. Many more defeats than victories, many low points. In other words wasted effort and time, but wasted only at first sight."

But Korczak points to Nietzsche's sad end and contrasts it with his own approaching death that he nevertheless still interprets in a joyful way.

> "Around me there are flowers and butterflies and glowworms and the concert of the crickets and the soloist in the high heavens – the Lark.
> Merciful God. I thank you, merciful God for the meadow and the sunset, for the fresh air in the evening after a hot day of effort and labor.
> Merciful God who has made everything so wisely that the flowers sent, that the glowworms light the earth, that the stars sparkle in the sky.
> How joyful old age is..." (SW 15, 299).

The thankfulness that is nourished by memories from the past – there were no meadows in the ghetto – still allow Korczak, despite the dark times, to speak of joy in life. Life is a good gift, a prayer of thanks changes our view of life and the world.

## 8 Perspective in Dark Times

Janusz Korczak wanted to give his children God and the possibility of prayer as a perspective on life.

"How childish is the hope of parents (just don't call it progressive) that one can ease a child's understanding of the world that surrounds them by telling them that there is no God. If there is no God then what is there? Who made everything? What will there be when I am dead? Where did the first human come from? Is it true that we simply live like animals if we do not pray? Father says that there are no angels, but I saw one with my own eyes. If it is not a sin, then why shouldn't we kill?" (SW 4, 107)

There are questions that neither teachers nor parents can answer — questions that have to remain unanswered.

Korczak's colleagues always insisted that the pedagogue was not religious. It is certain that Korczak did not follow a certain religion, and he did not want to have one under any circumstances. But, Korczak wanted to give the children a supportive and reliable life perspective. In the farewell prayer to the adolescents from the orphanage he said: "We give you one thing: a passion for a better life that is not possible but which may exist in the future, for a life of truth and justice. Maybe this passion will lead you to God and to a fatherland and to love. Fare well. Don't forget it" (SW 13, 370).

The combination of God and fatherland, which is so strange to us today, is made more palatable by the words about truth and justice. Children, people, need an orientation that they cannot find from within themselves and which cannot be imposed upon them, but one that they have to find for themselves. During the introduction of a religious service in Dom Sierot during the ghetto years of 1941 and 1942 Korczak gave a pointer towards orientation: "In these special times I believe that a religious service in Dom Sierot is urgently necessary. Prayer can give people courage in such tragic moments as we experience today."[24] In any case something supports people and gives a solid ground.

# 9 To Pray in Order to Withstand

God's story weaves people into a new reality. That is how human prayer works. God's call interrupts human limitation and resignation, fear and

---

24 Beiner, Janusz Korczak, Themen seines Lebens. (fn 6) 252 quoted in M. Zylberberg, In der Chlodna-Straße 33, in F. Beiner/S. Ungermann (Eds), Janusz Korczak in der Erinnerung, 512.

hopelessness. In the old Psalms, we read that those who pray do so in their most grave moments with the ancient prayer: "my God, my God, why have You forsaken me?" Their calls did not go unanswered. Heaven is here on earth when people need to call out, and when their own situation can only be understood not as a reflection of their own possibilities, but of God's.

A teacher's prayer is told to us by Janusz Korczak:

> "I do not have a long prayer, oh God. I do not send sigh after sigh … I bow in deepest humility, bring no costly sacrifice in order to praise you and to honor you. I have no desire to ingratiate myself into your powerful grace…My thoughts do not have wings to carry my song up into heaven.
>
> My words have neither perfume nor color nor are they flowery. I am tired, and I am exhausted.
>
> My sight is weak, and my back is bent under the heavy burden of my responsibilities.
>
> And yet I pray to you from deep within, oh God. And yet I have a treasure that I do not wish to share with my brother – with humanity. I am afraid that others will not understand, not empathize, not respect me, that they will laugh at me.
>
> If I stand before you in great humility, o Lord, in my plea I stand, indeed, as if with flaming demand. Even if I whisper quietly, this plea I speak with the voice of undependable will. I send my order to you, flaming through the clouds.
>
> I make this demand with my head held high because it is not for me. Give the children a good future, support them when they try and bless their efforts.
>
> You need not guide them on the easiest path but on the most beautiful.
>
> In exchange, I offer you my only treasure: my sadness. My sadness and labor."
> (SW 5, 68)

Is that a prayer? It reads like a request, unashamedly demanding, reaching up like Job. It is a fight: all worries, all fears become a demand. Who has the right to make such demands? Perhaps people no longer know God. The childlike idea of a god who fulfills their wishes has long been left behind. But what is known is that we have neither ourselves nor our lives in our own hands. There is an Other to whom we owe our lives. This Other carries us — the children too. I am not the creator, but I am also not fate. I can call out. The call does not go out to fate but to God, who nevertheless holds both me and the children in his hands.

Did he not promise himself when he promised the gift of life? We can give adolescents the opportunity to cry out to God at any time. The discussion about whether there is a God then becomes unimportant.

Can parents, can teachers pray and plead for their children in other ways than the praying educator in the above quoted prayer? The educators must let the children go, in contrast to the educators assumed own "universal responsibility".

## 10  Why?

"My God, my God, why hast thou forsaken me?" That is the God to whom people can cry out when they can no longer pray.

Parents and teachers are not in command – God be thanked – of their children's and pupils' beliefs. But it is painful if people lose their connection to God, regardless of whether it is an angry departure or simply absentmindedness because other things become more important.

But God waits, and he comes to our thoughts, as Emmanuel Lévinas says. Sudden memories emerge of this marginal figure, this God, who is more than everything. Perhaps he looked over and took care of your childhood, as a father, as all-knowing, as a protector or even as a chastiser. The question is whether memories of these concepts come back to life and can win our confidence, so that out of the distant God a close God arrives who can accompany us. We can cry out in the night and in times of need, when we are alone and unhappy, and we can celebrate, happy with joy and liberation. The experience of the Psalms becomes real: "He reached down from heaven and rescued me; he drew me out of deep waters." (Psalms 18:17)

In the Warsaw ghetto, Korczak wrote in his diary: "My life has been difficult but interesting. In my youth I asked God for a life like this. 'Give me, oh Lord, a difficult but beautiful, rich and worthy life.'" (SW 15, 360) Life, even a difficult one, is a gift. God — the Other of the question "Why?" for which there can be no answer. But next to him who prays, there stands a consoler.

# 7 Dying – Death — Finitude

## 1 Incomprehensible

The experience of dying, death and finitude is also part of the child's life, every day. Beloved animals die. Children also hear about the death of unknown people. Friends have accidents, including a child from the kindergarten. Fear gets around. The parents are sad because a good friend has died. A young father has died of a serious illness. Can this be understood? How are we to comprehend this? Does everyone die? Where are they when they are dead? Are they buried or are they in heaven?

The question about where the dead are is an attempt to grasp the incomprehensibility of the finitude of life. We cannot imagine the end of our time, and the end of someone we love cannot be comprehended by anyone. For this reason we hang an afterwards onto the timeline, as if the line was eternal. Where are the dead? In Paradise? We know the story. "We can ride on lions there," says a four year old. We can imagine it. Paradise — a mysterious place described in biblical tradition. "What will the angels say if the three of us (he and his parents) arrive together?" That was a three year old boy's question to his parents. He had heard of death but could not imagine being separated from them. People who love each other have to die together. That is why the outraged question was posed when a child at kindergarten died in a car crash: "Why did her mother not die with her?" Incomprehensible!

The whole world collapses when death plays its role. Fear spreads. Children, by nature, do not believe that life can simply end, that we can simply say, "it's over." A human lifespan is finite, but we cannot say with certainty, "it's over." Our understanding of life rebels against it.

Where is my friend now? He can't simply no longer exist. The "no longer" of a person we have loved is unthinkable. In our memories, in our love, in our thoughts, they are still here. Life cannot simply have been snuffed out.

Fear is where death and the afterlife do not emanate from life but from terrifying fantasies. We can fantasize about hell, and we know of the many hells that people impose on each other.

## 2 Loneliness

A real, threatening hell for children is separation and being left alone. That is why children try to ensure that they will not die alone and without their toys. It is a promise that consoles them. "Can I take my toys with me?" Again and again, a five year old plagued with this fear will ask this question in order to receive the same promise, again and again, that there will be no separation in death. Love preserves and connects everything. And a mother can answer the child's fearful question quite honestly, "Of course you can take everything that you love with you." We must not torture the child in this situation with the threat of "I don't know."

"Take everything with me" must be a great comfort against the thought of being alone. Take everything: the cars, the books, the figures and building blocks, everything. Does the young boy count up his things, because he himself is no more secure in his own concept of death? Only later do other concepts emerge: the hand that takes his, the voice that consoles. There is music that can help against being alone. A four-year-old child who is separated from its mother for an extended time always goes to sleep with a particular piece of music. The music is associated with safety and protection, as well as the presence of the mother. The compulsion to take everything with us can change. A sense of being supported and cared for emerges. Trust and love reach out beyond the destruction of all relationships.

But new fears emerge. Like a monster they creep into everything. Only a reliable presence helps against the power of fear. That is why it takes so much time to accompany children on their life's journey. A mother sits next to her child's bed in the evening because her mere presence helps against fear. And what if fear cannot be driven out? Together fear can be endured. Fear shared gives rise to trust. Somebody is with me. I am not alone.

## 3 Hell

Janusz Korczak tells of an experience with death when he was five years old. He wanted to bury his dead canary, packed in cotton wool in a sweet tin, under the chestnut tree in the courtyard.

> "I wanted to put a cross on its grave, but the maid said no, it was a bird, something of much lower status than a human. Even to cry would be a sin.

So much for the maid. Actually, what was much worse was the fact that the caretaker's son thought that the canary was Jewish. Like me. I was also a Jew, but he was a Pole, a Catholic. He would go to heaven. I, on the other hand - and as long as I didn't use any indecent expressions and stole sugar at home and brought it to him like an obedient servant — I would go somewhere after my death that wasn't exactly hell, but it would be dark there. And I was afraid of a darkened room.
Death. A Jew. Hell. A dark Jewish paradise. More than enough to make me think." (SW 15, 301f.)

Social and religious distortions are connected and dangerously reinforced by images of hell. Children experience places of fear, whether we call them hell or not. Are we able to give them the courage to stand against this fear? Healthy relationships will protect them against being overcome with fear.

Wolf Erlbruch relates a conversation between a duck and death. The duck says: "Some ducks say that deep under the earth there is a hell where ducks are roasted if they haven't been good." Death replies, in all ignorance: "What extraordinary things you ducks tell each other – but who knows?"[25] For a child, this is a deadly serious matter, and it does not recognize the consoling humor in the joke.

# 4 What Help is there Against Fear?

One antidote to fear is the question as to whether God has toys in heaven. But an affirmative answer only helps so far. Erlbruch tells another idea that is often brought to bear this situation: "Some ducks say that you become an angel and sit on a cloud and look down at the earth." Death responds: "That's entirely possible. You do have wings after all." But this cynical consolation may well provoke the response that we do not wish to live on clouds but on the earth. We recognize this kind of talk from Ludwig Thoma's Münchener im Himmel. As far as death is concerned, no matter how one looks at it, there is no consolation.

Parents and teachers try to defeat fear by distracting their children. A six-year-old who already has good mathematical ability counts against fear. "How long do we live? When do we die?" The years are counted up: 2000, 2010, 20, 30… 2100, and then, finally, comes the question: "Will my children still

---

25 Wolf Erlbruch, Ente, Tod Tulpe, Munich 2007.

be alive then?" Life becomes a chain of numbers. The question of "where?" is replaced by the question of "when?" Ancient apocalyptic calculations also attempt an answer to this question. Does this remove the threat?

Answers that are designed on the basis of calculating time: not today, but later, can only help for a short while. There can be no victory over fear of death on some sort of timeline, because time will always catch you up.

Life is the only consolation against death. To understand life is to find a foothold, and life is to be found in the relationships we build in life. Love and trust can keep us safe in our fear. This is why Korczak, until the very last, was so careful about the way they lived even in the dreadful conditions of Dom Sierot during the times of the ghetto. It was only within order that consideration and care could be applied to the great number of children. Only within order, even in the most restricted space and threatened time, could there be life and connection: respect, duty, play, fairy tales, art, music, meals together – even when there was not much to eat — prayer and religious service, caring for the sick. Alongside the threats to life, these things gave a sense of safety. It is only in our relationships that we stand against the threat of the great break that death represents.

Korczak's concept of life determined his relationship to death and dying people in the ghetto. He says: "When, in the darkest moments, I weighed up the possibility of killing babies and older people in the Jewish ghetto (euthanasia) who were doomed to die I saw that that would be murder, murder of the sick and the weak and the unknowing." (SW 15, 358) Korczak also approached the head of the Health Department of the Jewish Council (in the ghetto) to make sure that any children dying in the streets were taken in and given a room:

> "If we can't save their lives, then at least we can guarantee them a humane, decent death. We don't need a lot of space for that, and it doesn't involve great cost. We need only a large room, with shelves, like in a haberdashery." (SW 15, 255, fn. 1)

In shared life together, it is not only children who are given a foothold and hope in uncertain times. It is not religiosity, but life that resists death and fear. It was said of Korczak that he was not religious, but he knew how to nourish life. In that sense, he stood entirely within the biblical tradition. The face that sends its light down and is never turned away is the epitome of a good life: "The Lord makes his face to shine upon you, and be gracious to you." This is the Aaronic blessing in the 4th Book of Moses (Numbers 6:25).

There are parents who send their children off in the morning with a beaming smile, setting them up for the day. This smile, too, is like a blessing, a supportive power. There are symbols in life that represent the durability of a relationship. Respect and forgiveness when mistakes are made, again and again, is an experience of life and love that strengthens us against the power of death. There is no door that is shut forever. That is our experience of relationships that endure. Again and again there is respect and forgiveness. This is a consolation of a sort only a mother can know. The Bible tells us that God represents this sort of consolation. That is our experience of life against death. These experiences precede our knowledge of Christian belief, which tells us that at the lowest point of human existence, someone is there for us, protecting us against the fear of death. I think that the experience of acceptance, love, forgiveness and consolation goes deep into the heart of children and gives them strength until the end of their lives.

When, in August 1942, Janusz Korczak was being pushed into the wagons, together with the children of the orphanage, to be transported from Warsaw station, the German commandant, who knew his children's books, offered to allow him to stay behind. Korczak went back to the children in the dark wagons. That was how he did justice to the children. By holding onto the children, redemptive justice – which holds all humans in its hands – was exercised. It is in justice that the concept of the far away God comes near. He carries us through the fear of death to new life.

We cannot invent fantastic stories at the end of life about what is to come next. They do not work. The wiping away of tears and of becoming new is experienced here and now in life, and we also know that this happens against everything that life shows us. That is how a three and half year old girl can say with complete conviction that "God makes it so that we only die when we want to die." That is a childlike trust in life to the very end and beyond. All we can do is agree.

Janusz Korczak did not offer the children refuge in an afterlife or another world. He lived justice, this vibrant power that, in the biblical tradition, describes the intact relationship between people, between God and people and between God and nature, here and now, not in some speculative other world but in the here and now of every day. We have to live with children in the here and now, with full presence. God's eternity illuminates it and reaches out beyond its boundaries.

# 8 Once Again on Bringing up Children

## 1 To What Purpose?

If we ask what is the purpose of it all, then the point of both life and education is missed because life is its own purpose. To live with children and to bring them up has its own purpose. Point and purpose do not exist in some imaginary place in which our development is towards the end of or beyond our lives. If point and purpose are removed from our lives and relocated to a place beyond us, then we suffer harm. Children are then seen as "incomplete people", as deficient creatures that still have to be formed. The right to life is reduced because, as children, they are seen as incomplete people.

But children are people just as they are now; Janusz Korczak never stopped maintaining this. Children are made from dust but contain God. To think of the biblical tradition is to remind us that a child does not belong to us. It is not our property but exists as God's creation. This demands respect and a recognition that children must not be formed according to the will and plan of the educator. As part of creation, they have worth from the very beginning, without preconditions and stand not only in relation to you but are gifts to themselves from an Other from which they draw succor, to which they pray and express their wishes. They are not limited to finitude.

It is a terrible crime to form children according to our own educational wishes and our own ideals. You may wish to create a person according to your ideas of how a child should be. "And you look for an ideal to which it should conform. You dream of a life for your child." (SW 4, 13). How often this leads to a distortion of any concept of freedom because a child does not conform. Children look for their own lives, not for lives thought out and desired by you. Of course, both parents and educators exist as models. At first children behave in ways that they learn from their parents and others with whom they live.

If, however, they are brought up to be independent and have critical insight, they will be in a position later to choose for themselves, to become who they are. "I thank you that I am a proper person." This formulation comes from the tradition of a belief in creation at the foundation of which belongs the right of the child to become what it is.

Time and again we see ideal conceptions of upbringing promulgated. In the 19th century, German idealism developed as its educational goal the mature, complete personality. Maturity, completeness of personality, was seen as the goal of the education of an individual. This ideal continued until well into the 20th century and still exists today everywhere where education is dominated by the concept of a harmonious and complete personality. Ideals are not only alien educational concepts but are often uniforms in which children have to become what their parents or teachers want them to.

Other times and other ideologies create other ideals and other prison uniforms. The socialist personality, the disciplined little soldier who is to march only for its fatherland or the ideal of the fully integrated person who carries out all rules and regulations, thereby guaranteeing a comfortable life are two examples of this. A consumer society with almost unlimited desires and possibilities also creates a uniform into which children are to fit. Education is designed to serve this end. But for what purpose?

Korczak's third right of the child: "the child has a right to be what it is", stands against all educational ideals. A child should be and is allowed to be itself, a proper person, standing freely amongst its fellow individuals. With its fears and wishes, it can go beyond its parents and teachers and turn to an Other. This freedom is the concrete experience of God, concrete here and now in its own life. The power of the child's self grows out of its desires and prayers, although not all of its wishes are by any means fulfilled.

## 2 The Primacy of the Present

Janusz Korczak's second right of the child is "the child's right to today". This right, too, is a challenge for parents and educators, at least when education means not to live together, but to achieve certain goals. Of course children learn and can achieve extraordinary things. They can also achieve their goals in physical and intellectual pursuits in many different areas. But is that all that a life with children is to contain? Should an ability to perform, as much as we all desire it, be the only thing that determines life?

Performance is orientated towards the future. If life is reduced only to achieving performative goals, then today, the present, is only ever seen as a passing stage towards a higher goal. The present loses its force, and today loses its value, because it is reduced to a point on the road towards a greater goal. Life is then no longer a meadow that one can enjoy and over which rainbows can be seen but becomes like a race track on which we have to fight. This is an image which speaks to the life experiences of many, as does the idea of a "racetrack" to death which Andreas Gryphius used to illustrate the transience of life in his poem "Evening". With the metaphor of the meadow, Korczak points to the experience of joy at a gifted life and to the experience of thankfulness. Gifted life provokes the present here and today so that God's being in time can be concretely experienced.

## 3  Religious Education?

"We cannot live without belief." So said the young Janusz Korczak (SW 3, 82). According to the understanding of belief as it exists in the biblical tradition, i.e. belief as trust and courage then this is true. People need trust, trust in life and courage. Can children be taught this? In living with each other in daily life, belief can come about, as can prayer, even though belief and prayer are not present as such. The trust that we gain through prayer can be found in everyday life. But if belief becomes just the collection of unquestioned religious regulations, and prayer becomes just pious compulsion, then we may well be able to force something onto a child, but the disappointment that results, when young people turn away from all aspects of religion, hits teachers and parents hard.

Belief cannot be the object of education or religious training. Belief is lived, and it carries life. It is as not available as life itself. Nevertheless, belief and religious education are instrumentalized time and again in the development of the individual. The liberating power of belief and the joy provoked by trusting life get lost in this development. The freedom of a Christian who lives from the love that God provides becomes an educational ideal. The freedom: you are allowed to live becomes the constraint: you must live.

How can we speak of God in our life together with children? Where life is spoken of, so God, too, is spoken of. Religious upbringing leads us to life, to God and to the world. God is to be found in life, and in the world, he shows himself as a secret. Parents and educators should not provide lessons in religion or spread specialist knowledge. In our lives with children, there should be no theoretical expositions about God. But people live in God's story, even if they do not realize it. We have to admit to ourselves that children also grow and develop if their parents and educators do not know about God. But God is concrete in our lives. He is with people whether they know it or not. We can tell stories about God, life stories that liberate us and give us courage. Janusz Korczak is constantly hinting at this when he talks about thankfulness in life and experience, when joy is expressed, or lamentation; when wonder is provoked and when, at the center of our lives together, forgiveness exists. That happened every day in Dom Sierot, even before the terrible times of 1941 when regular church services were introduced.

Thankfulness, joy, lamentation, wonder and forgiveness — these are the arrows which direct us towards God's story, which is told of in the many ancient verses of the books of the Bible and the tradition of belief. These stories allow something of the experience of gifted life to come to us in the present. Life is not just a daily chore but rather points to the life and times of God's being in time. Education and upbringing can be understood as a life with children within God's story, in which life is gifted to us and preserved in time and space. Thankfulness, joy and lamentation are the answer to this – responsibility, suffering and fear are contained within this story. If we trust in this story, we can understand the right of the child to die. Parents and educators must carefully lead a child, but the biblical God encompasses both life and death.

# Bibliography

Korczak, Janusz, Sämtliche Werke, Ed. von Friedhelm Beiner and Erich Dautzenroth, Vols 1–16, Gütersloher Verlagshaus, Güterloh, 1996–2005.

Korczak, Janusz, Beichte eines Schmetterlings, 1892–1895, SW, Vol. 3, 59–131.

Korczak, Janusz, Wenn ich wieder klein bin, SW, Vol. 3, 133–276.

Korczak, Janusz, Wie liebt man ein Kind, SW, Vol. 4, 9–318.

Korczak, Janusz, Erziehungsmomente, SW, Vol. 4, 319–382.

Korczak, Janusz, Das Recht des Kindes auf Achtung, SW, Vol. 4, 383–414.

Korczak, Janusz, Fröhliche Pädagogik, SW, Vol. 4, 415–493.

Korczak, Janusz, Der Frühling und das Kind, SW, Vol. 5, 7–28.

Korczak, Janusz, Allein mit Gott, SW, Vol. 5, 29–68.

Korczak, Janusz, Frühe Texte über Kinder und Erziehung, SW, Vol. 9, 15–158.

Korczak, Janusz, Theorie und Praxis der Erziehung (1923–1939), SW, Vol. 9, 237–370.

Korczak, Janusz, Die Burse und ich, SW 9, 487–539.

Korczak, Janusz, Eindrücke und Notizen aus Sommerkolonien, SW, Vol. 10, 7–72.

Korczak, Janusz, Ruhm (1913), SW, Vol. 10, 261–302.

Korczak, Janusz, Berichte und Geschichten aus den Waisenhäusern. Aus dem Dom Sierot 1913–1926, SW, Vol. 13, 311–482.

Korczak, Janusz, Reglement und Organisationsstruktur der Waisenhäuser, SW, Vol. 13, 541–563.

Korczak, Janusz, Dokumente aus den Kriegs- und Ghettojahren, SW, Vol. 15, 147–294.

Korczak, Janusz, Tagebuch – Erinnerungen (1942), SW, Vol. 15, 295–377.

Argelander, Hermann, Der Flieger. Eine charakteranalytische Fallstudie, Suhrkamp, Frankfurt am Main 1985.

Beiner, Friedhelm, Was Kindern zusteht. Janusz Korczaks Pädagogik der Achtung. Inhalt-Methoden - Chancen, Gütersloher Verlagshaus, Gütersloh 2008, 100f.

Beiner, Friedhelm, Janusz Korczak, Themen seines Lebens. Eine Werkbiographie, Gütersloher Verlagshaus, Gütersloh, 2011.

Erlbruch, Wolf, Ente, Tod und Tulpe, Antje Kunstmann, München 2007.

Falska, Maria, Umriß der Organisation der Erziehungsarbeit im 'Nasz Dom', (SW 13, 547–563).

Jüngel, Eberhard, "Gott ist ein Rufwort (Mk 15, 34)." Ders. - Gott - als Wort unserer Sprache (1969), in: Ders. Unterwegs zur Sache. Theologische Bemerkungen, Mohr (Paul Siebeck), Tübingen, 2000[3], 80–104, 97.

Ricoeur, Paul, Zeit und Erzählung, Vol. 1, Zeit und historische Erzählung, Aus dem Französischen von Rainer Rochlitz, Wilhelm Fink Verlag, München 1988. (Original P. Ricoeur, Temps et récit, Paris 1983).

Rosenzweig, Franz, Briefe und Tagebücher. Vol 2, Haag: Nijhoff 1979.

Sandel, Michael, J., The Case Against Perfection, The Belknap Press of Havard University Press, Harvard 2007.

Sartre, Jean-Paul, The Words, New York, 1964.

Sennett, Richard, Respekt im Zeitalter der Ungleichheit, Berlin Verlag, Berlin 2007[2] (Original: R. Sennett, Respect in a World of Inequality, W. W. Norton, New York 2002).

Schneider-Flume, Gunda, Leben ist kostbar. Wider die Tyrannei des gelingenden Lebens, Vandenhoeck und Ruprecht, Göttingen 2008[3].

Ungermann, Silvia, Die Pädagogik Janusz Korczaks. Theoretische Grundlegung und praktische Verwirklichung 1896–1942, Gütersloher Verlagshaus, Gütersloh 2006.